LONDON

646

O CIRCS EX FISHLOCK

TAN

publican
25 April 81

a humble place, low and dark, but
ter ▓ a day in the mountains. It
straw strewn on it, and wood-framed
mud walls. There was no flue, so
fire filled the room and pricked the
~~moments~of~arrival~than~was~~

rooms which travellers can claim
the rugged parts of Afghanistan.
raditional~~~~~~ OF PROVIDING
~Exchange~and~the~credit~
~k~z~b~r~k~t~e~r~z~w~a~x~f~n~e~x~a~s~
question of payment.
irsty and weary when I
But within a few mo

hanistan.
C YDL839
LDT
PROTELENEWS MANGO 1 EXDELHI:
ROBERRY FEATURES EXFISHLOCK DELHI AUGU
THE VOLUPTUOUS MANGO. IT IS THE ONE COMPE
FOR THE FIERCE BLAZE OF THE EARLY INDIAN SUMMER AN
RAISING HEAT OF THE MONSOON THAT FOLLOWS. SHOWERS AND THE SHA
OF TREES AND BRIEF COOLNESS AT DAWN PROVIDE THEIR WELCOME
REFRESHMENT, SOLACE AND RELIEF (SEMI) BUT AS A REWARD FOR
ENDURING SUMMER'S TYRANNY NOTHING COMPARES WITH THE FRUIT WH
IS A NATIONAL PASSION.
MANGO EATING IS SUCH A SENSUOUS PLEASURE THAT INDIANS
THAT A MAN TIRED OF MANGOES IS TIRED OF LIFE. CERTAINLY
KNOW THEIR MANGOES. THEY HAVE CULTIVATED THEM FOR FOUR T
YEARS. TODAY INDIA PRODUCES MORE THAN SEVEN TENTHS OF T
CROP AND INDIAN MANGOES ARE INDISPUTABLY THE FINEST.
THEY COME IN MORE THAN A THOUSAND VARIETIES AND EACH HAS IT
DISTINCTIVE SCENT, SWEETNESS, SPICINESS AND TEXTURE, THE COLOUR
OF THE FLESH RANGING FROM PALE YELLOW TO GORGEOUS ORANGE. MANGO
NOISSEURS, WHO HAVE MUCH IN CO~~ ~~ ~~ WITH SKILLED STUDENTS OF
~~AN TELL BY SHAPE, SKIN, P~~ ~~ ~~ ~~ ~~ THE DISTRICT,
~~RCHARD, A MANGO COMES ~~ ~~ ~~ ~~ ~~ TELL THE
~~ DARE YOU TO DIS~~

174 TELLON 6
RO DAILY TELEGRAPH

PRO OP-ED

EXFISHLOCK, DELHI, FE

TAKE ONE WHISKERS

IN PUNJAB TODAY A MAN'
STRANGE POLITICS OF BEARDS
THE GROWTH THE BETTER. HIND
FORM OF PROTECTION- AND A S

WHEN SIKH TERRORISTS STOPPED A BUS THEY SORTED THE PAS
INTO HINDUS AND SIKHS AND STARTED SHOOTING THE HINDU MEN
THEIR EYES FELL A BOY OF 18 IN THE
HER WHO HAD A BEARD AND TURBAN.
FATHER'S PLEADINGS TH
THROUGH THE HEAD.

HAVE AN IMPORTAN
LAY A CURIOUS
THEY ARE THE

D0295803

SI. No. 160
FUNERAL OF SHRI RAJIV GANDHI
FORMER PRIME MINISTER
PRESS
MAY 24, 1991
Name
Organisation   Principal Info

JULIO
Trelew
Pto.
Madryn
o Viceversa
Serie 2
673

PRESS
FUNDIR
RONALD REAGAN FORSETA
OG
MIKHAIL GORBACHEV ADALRITARA
Í REYKJAVÍK 11–12 OKT. 1986
TREVOR FISHLOCK
DAILY TELEGRAPH
UK
ΠΡΕССА
№ 1147

PRESS INFORMATION BUREAU
GOVT. OF INDIA
PRESS
CORRESPONDENT
TEMPORARY
TREVOR FISHLOCK
The Sunday Telegraph
British
VALID UPTO
18.5.93
26
Principal Information Officer

FIRSTAIR
YFB
IQALUIT
(FROBISHER BAY)
110283

HELSINKI SUMMIT
9.9.1990
JOURNALIST
Fishlock
Trevor
Daily Telegraph

ROYAL VISIT
TO AUSTRALIA
r Fishlock
SYMBOL

a big Mi124 gu hip
, and everywhere I
g to bring them down." They

RAF
FI

ACC. No: 02933065
24-02-51

TREVOR FISHLOCK
Reporter

TREVOR FISHLOCK
Reporter

Gomer

First published in 2017 by Gomer Press,
Llandysul, Ceredigion SA44 4JL

ISBN 978 1 78562 052 2
A CIP record for this title is available from the British Library.

This book is published with the financial support of the
Welsh Books Council.

Printed and bound in Wales at
Gomer Press, Llandysul, Ceredigion
www.gomer.co.uk

For Penny
Richard and Tim

Contents

Chapter 1

Any news in the paper?

In the age before television, my father and mother read the daily news as happy as horses with nosebags. Among the crumpled pages at their feet I breathed the inky tang and headline lingo of the time: spiv and smog and Skylon, teddy boy, cold war, prefab, ration book, H-bomb, iron curtain, eleven-plus, Korea, Churchill, Eisenhower.

Groundnuts and Bradman's duck.

As they turned the pages, Dad liked to read a sentence or two aloud. His armchair's broken spring pinged a protest as he shifted his weight. 'Listen to this,' he said, and Mum always listened and said: 'Fancy that.'

Sometimes he adopted his special grim voice.

'Here's another one for the eight o'clock walk.'

The papers cost a penny or two. Three dropped daily on our doormat. On Sundays, there was the *News of the World*. Dad filed it behind a cushion.

On 6 February 1952, my mother ran upstairs to my room where I was weathering a childhood pox. She had just heard the news on the wireless and stood framed and dramatic in the doorway.

'The king is dead.'

Next day the papers fell thick and black. I foraged in the pages and studied every detail in the photographs. Later there was the lying in state, the catafalque, the soldiers' rifles reversed, heads bowed, three queens in black with faces veiled. The newsreels at the Regal showed it all.

We were living in Hayling Island. My father's name was Edward, forever Ted. He had black hair and hazel eyes. My mother's name was Ada. She was blue-eyed and fair. I have their studio engagement photograph. My father wore an overcoat and gloves, his trilby slightly tilted. My mother perched on a stool beside him, her ankles crossed. She wore a cloche hat, a coat, and gloves and shiny stockings.

All his life my father remained loyal to the habits he embraced in his long service in the Royal Marines. He stood close to his razor in the morning and sat often for the barber. He was devoted to the corps. He taught me the motto: *Per Mare Per Terram*, the first Latin I knew. He took pride in his voice. In his seniority, he was a regimental sergeant major. His leonine parade ground roar shrivelled marines at a hundred yards. Most of all, however, he loved to take the stage and sing. His bass-baritone was resonant and rich and he had confidence. He performed at concerts and shows, at regimental dinners and hospitals and, once or twice, at a prison.

For years, he retained a wartime respect for the BBC news. 'Quiet, you boys,' he said, switching on the old wireless by his chair. The valves warmed up and chiselled voices commanded the room. We sat fixed in concentration. *HMS Amethyst* dashed down the Yangtze under fire, 1949. The Portsmouth-based submarine *Affray* sank with all hands, 1951. The *Flying Enterprise* foundered, 1952. Dad followed the fighting in Korea, so we heard of Imjin and the 38th parallel without much understanding. But we knew of Big Bill Speakman who won the VC.

My father still had a bit of pull after his retirement from the Royal Marines. He treated me to a trip in a DUKW landing craft. It growled its way down a slipway and splashed thrillingly into the sea, Dad revelling in the spray and motion. 'Big time stuff, eh?' he said. This was his accolade for any adventurous entertainment. The films of John Wayne were always big time stuff.

When Dr Brennan came with his black bag and Mum gave me slippery junket and Virol and covered my chest with Thermogene, I read the days away. Dad gave me *The Adventures of Tom Sawyer*, so wonderful that on reaching the last word I returned at once to the first. It led the way to *Huckleberry Finn*. The exploits of Biggles, William Brown and the teams of schoolboy heroes slid down like Popeye's can of spinach. Meanwhile, I helped myself to Mum's book club delivery. She read far more books than my father and all the days of her life began with the newspapers. She lived to be 100 and kept her wits to the end.

The book club sent *Our Dearest Emma*, the story of Nelson's mistress. I knew of Nelson because Dad took me to see *HMS Victory*, an excursion pretty well obligatory for any boy in Portsmouth. I read Nevil Shute's *No Highway* and *A Town Like Alice* simply because Shute lived and wrote for some years in a nearby house-in-the-woods called Pond Head. I imagined him scrolling the paper into his typewriter and lighting a pipe, which, surely, all real authors did. In *A Town Like Alice* I discovered Australia. I knew Pond Head because a friend lived there. His parents were rich. His train set filled a room. We played cricket on the lawn, and when it rained we played his mother's pianola. On sunny days, she sat on a terrace with a jug of exotic drink. 'Pimm's,' she said, when I asked.

The quinqueremes of Christmas rowed home to haven with heavyweight golden treasuries, epics of knights and of willowy princesses with hair like flowing waterfalls. I never forgot A P Herbert's comic poem:

> The doctor took my shirt away,
> He did it for the best,
> He said, 'It's very cold today,'
> And took away my vest,
> Then, having nothing more to say,
> He hit me in the chest.

Illustrations in adventure annuals depicted teenage boys wearing ties and neatly-parted barbered hair. They cried 'Great Scott,' and always felled their foes in the English way, 'a smart uppercut to the jaw'. Ripping yarns in the *Wizard* and *The Hotspur* unfolded in grey, biblical columns. We had *John Bull* every week and *Picture Post*'s mirror of the real world.

The encyclopedia I had when I was eight was a marvel. It remains so, the edges of its pages worn and blackened by my thumbing, its spine supported by tape. It still teaches science, literature, art, astronomy, music, histories and praise for famous men. Where else could I have read the life of Garibaldi or have seen Horatius defending the Tiber bridge, a picture I copied often in my drawings? Illustrations of human innards were useful then and remain so now. The picture of the digestive system shows the large intestine, the end of the road. A man waits nearby, ready with a dustbin on his back.

The first words in the encyclopedia were these: 'The memory of the war is very close to all of us today. Most of us had relatives who were in the Navy, the Army or the Air Force. Many were killed or wounded; many more men, women and children were killed by bombs in their homes or at work. Few of the children who lived in England, France, Germany and other European countries will have forgotten the air raids.'

Portsmouth endured sixty-seven raids. These killed more than 1,000 people in the city. My earliest memory is of my mother carrying me into a shelter. I remember the grey siren suit she made for me, its red piping. Alone in a raid, she gave birth to my brother. Our cityscape was of rubble mounds, weeds and wild flowers, eviscerated houses, great timber props shoring blackened walls, tiers of fireplaces but no floors.

★

In the early years of the twentieth century my father's father, Herbert, quit the plough in Wiltshire and sought his fortune. As many men did, he went to the collieries of the booming valleys of southern Wales, the greatest source of energy in the world. He found work at the coalface in the Albion colliery, near Pontypridd. At a Pontypridd church in 1905, he married Lily Williams, a florist from the village of Nantymoel. My father was born a year later.

Herbert was adventurous, romantic and restless. In 1912 he bought a third-class steamer ticket to Australia. In the year he spent there, he worked and travelled, and returned with his heart set on an Australian life for his family. He had found his exciting future. On the last leg of his journey, heading home to Pontypridd, he paused in Cardiff to buy a ring for Lily.

As an army reservist in the Somerset Light Infantry he was called up early in August 1914. My father watched him eat the breakfast Lily cooked. He remembered the two eggs on his father's plate. Usually there was only one. He saw that one of his Dad's boots was shiny and the other not, perhaps because of drinks the evening before.

Within a month, Herbert was fighting at Le Cateau on the western front. Five of his pencilled letters survive, written on tiny sheets. He asked Lily to send him pipe tobacco and his favourite newspapers, 'the News, Mail and Observer – they seem very homely to read'. Later he wrote: 'How about the Despatch occasionally Dear, it's my favourite Sunday newspaper.'

In another he wrote: 'I love you beyond all doubt, you are ever before me, and our dear kids, you must learn Ted and Howard not to forget me but speak of me sometimes.'

At the end of October, he wrote to Lily: 'I hope the Kaiser will die a right death for this trouble, well, dear, whenever I return I shall try and give the colliery a bye, perhaps go to Australia if you are willing. Now Dearest all I can say about myself is that I am quite well, but it is bitter cold at night.'

The white monument beside the road at Ploegsteert, near Ypres, with its leoglyphs and columns, honours more than 11,000 soldiers who had no known grave. Herbert's name is among them: he was killed on 9 November, aged twenty-nine. Dad was the only one of Herbert's four children who retained a memory of him and of his departure for the war. In a cinema in Pontypridd he saw a photograph of Herbert among pictures of other local men killed in action. I was about eight when I asked Dad about his father. I did not know he had been killed. Dad told me. It was the first time I saw his face creased by pain, the certain shadow of grief.

★

My mother's father, William, survived the trenches. When he came home, he walked sixty miles from Portsmouth to Haslemere in Surrey to find a job and a home for his family. I remember him, a tall and amiable man smoking a cigarette, leaning on a mantelpiece. He preferred to stand, Mum said, because his shrapnel wound made sitting uncomfortable. My mother's daily duty as a child was to put her younger brother to bed. She carefully lifted out his glass eye with a spatula and placed it in water, returning it to its socket in the morning before she left for school. Her brother died of diphtheria when he was twelve.

In 1926, as the Depression cloaked everything, Dad signed on for twenty-one years' service in the Royal Marines. He met Ada at a palais de danse in Portsmouth. It cost them fourpence each to get in and twopence a glass for lemonade. There was no bar and the band stopped at 11pm. For my mother and father, those were the romantic dancing years and for the rest of their lives they often talked of them. They married in Portsmouth in 1929, when he was twenty-three and she eighteen, he dashing in his dark blue uniform, she pretty in lace. In the following year, my sister was born. A brother and a sister born in the mid–1930s died in their infancy.

As a Royal Marine, my father served in three warships in the Mediterranean: the cruiser *Centaur*, the aircraft carrier *Courageous* and the battleship *Revenge*. It was the custom for Royal Marines to man one of the gun turrets. In my father's recollections, the royals were always smarter and quicker, ever ahead of the Royal Navy men. Years later, when we, his three sons, were growing up, he would growl if he caught any of us leaning a lazy buttock on the table. 'Stand up straight,' he said. 'Only sailors sit on tables.' In his time, he was a small arms instructor and a crack shot who won marksmanship medals at Bisley. To his great pleasure, he became president of the sergeants' mess. He said that when it came to the way a barracks should be run, he and the colonel always saw eye to eye.

The blitz of Portsmouth persuaded Dad to send Mum to tranquil refuge in Hereford in January 1941. I emerged a month later in my grandmother's little house by the lovely River Wye. My ten-year-old sister Norma was already there, an evacuee since 1940. When I was three months old Mum took both of us home to the red brick married quarters in the Royal Marines barracks. Years later, my sister told me that Mum said to Dad in a firm voice: 'We are a family and we should be together.'

And that was that.

Chapter 2

The holiday man

For my father, the ending of his twenty-one years in the Royal Marines was a bereavement. This was in 1947, the year of the great snows. He told me once that for a whole week he brooded and drank too much beer. Soon, however, he reinvented himself. Perhaps he shook off the blues with an extra haircut and an even closer shave. In any event, he reasoned that the sergeant major of a Royal Marines barracks could certainly be a holiday supremo. He became entertainment manager of the Coronation holiday camp in Hayling Island. Other holiday camps sported Redcoats. The Coronation had my father.

I was six when we went to Hayling. For me it was ever our island of adventure, flat and sandy, with an old steepled church, farms and meadows, woodlands and beaches. If you looked south from the spiky-grassed dunes you saw the eastern end of the Isle of Wight. A pugnacious little ferry butted its way from the crooked arm of south Hayling to Portsmouth. A small village had life's necessities, a W H Smith, a petrol station, some shops, a barber and hairdresser, and most importantly, the Regal cinema. My mother and father never learned to drive. They had bikes. We walked. But sometimes we had a lift in a car: how thrilling it was, the scent of leather and petrol.

The island was linked to the Hampshire coast by a weak wooden bridge. We children were decanted from the single-deck bus and walked across, heads down in the rain. Only a few stolid grandmas kept their seats. Our home at the holiday camp was a small house by a tidal creek and oyster beds. The boatmen of Chichester harbour puffed their pipes and took us out to see porpoises at play. From Thorney Island air force station came the bass drone of engines.

Dad's working rig was a yellow sports shirt, spacious slacks and a whistle on a cord. From the day he welcomed the first holidaymakers the camp was fully booked through the whole season. How families longed for the holiday. They left their burned and broken cities and arrived clutching the basic necessities: ration books, worn clothing and resurrected swimwear. Few men had the luxury of changing daily into a clean shirt. 'That first year,' my mother recalled, 'we lacked enough sheets for the chalet beds, so I cut every sheet in half and sewed a hem. They didn't fit but, of course, people were used to shortages and after years of war the camp was paradise.' And so it was.

The smart brick bungalows dated from the 1930s. The glamorous swimming pool was Mediterranean blue. Some men played in long whites on the tennis courts. A meadow had room for cricket, football, athletics and a sandpit. A reedy lake hosted swans, moorhens and boats. The campers enjoyed roller-skating, horse rides, two-seat tricycles, dining rooms, a ballroom, a theatre and bars and a river of beer. Dad knew that the old naval nickname for a Royal Marine was a Jolly, and jolly he would be. It was a roll-out-the-barrel holiday. He and the campers had shared wartime camaraderie, language and humour. Dad, being indefatigable, ran almost everything: the bathing beauty parade at the poolside, the knobbly knees contest, the ugly face competition, the tug-of-war, the fancy dress gala, athletics and swimming races. He played the clown in the water pageant and always fell from a boat with a splash.

Meanwhile, he restored mislaid false teeth, lost chalet keys and children to their owners. Ever the leader, he headed the weekly walk to a nearby country pub and told townie children not to eat deadly nightshade.

Early in the evening he called the tombola numbers. These were stamped on brass discs and Dad shook them up in a stiff canvas bag. We knew all the legs-eleven patter by heart. Dad called the last clickety-click and hurried home for a bath and a change into a suit or blazer.

After the campers' dinner, he compèred the variety show of comedians, conjurors, jugglers, ventriloquists, singers, siffleurs and resident jazzmen headed by the trumpeter Nat Gonella. The Deep River Boys, tall and slender singers from the American South, were the first Americans many of us had seen. Showgirls wore fishnets and glittering spangles or Edwardian music hall costumes with saucy frills. My brother and I saw more cancan than any boys in Britain.

On Thursdays Dad presented the campers' home-made talent show. He recruited my sister to sing *Apple Blossom Time* and *Ciribiribin*. My brother and I sang a comic duet taught by an ex-navy man called Nelson. It was our two minutes of limelight and ended with the lines:

> And what do you think we had for dinner?
> Pigeons' milk and nanny goat's liver.
> Go and tell your Aunt Maria, pussy's laid an egg.

Soon the pianist was rippling an intro and there was Dad striding on to the stage wearing his Royal Marines tie. He sang in the style of the balladeer Peter Dawson and his repertoire included *The Floral Dance, The Holy City, Old Father Thames* and *When the Sergeant Major's on Parade*:

> With Sam Browne belt and buttons bright
> Behold the Sergeant Major!

Dad admitted only two kinds of music, the human voice in glory and military bands which made tears shine on his cheek.

Mum wore her best on ballroom nights. 'Zip me up, dear,' she said, reaching for her sequinned purse. She hurried off to play Ginger Rogers to Dad's not quite Fred Astaire. Waltz, quickstep, foxtrot, they led the way, still revelling in their dancing. The glitter ball dappled the dancers, the band played *In the Mood* and Dad glided over the floor, ever nifty in his twinkling size eights.

★

For skinny boys as we were, scabby-kneed and brown as baps, Hayling was golden. Along our southern coast, we had beaches and grey wooden breakwaters to dive from, wartime concrete pillboxes to defend. First into the sea in spring, we were last out at summer's end and never late for tea. We roamed in copses and scrumpable orchards and had a tree house with a rope to swing on. A friend lived in the most marvellous home in the world, a railway carriage in a buttercup meadow.

No doubt our primary school was like most others: Victorian red brick, with coke stoves in the classrooms, white china inkwells in the stained desks, reeking wet mackintoshes in the lobby. Mr Earney, the headmaster, had been wounded in the first world war and his skull was repaired by a metal cap we called his silver plate. A devoted grey-haired Miss taught us reading, writing, times tables and the joy of stories. Vividly she described the air battles of the 1940s, vapour trails over the school, a parachute drifting down, children hurrying to the air raid shelters. Those turfed mounds were still there, crouched like armadillos beside the school.

We played games with the cardboard lids of our bottles of free milk. The best school lunch was corned beef hash, jam sponge and custard. Conker duels bruised our knuckles. Boys roared in piggyback wrestling. Girls gentled our condition with hopscotch. Bobby Tambling said I was hopeless at football. When his legs grew longer, he played for England.

Ours was a school of song. My earworms still sing *The Dashing White Sergeant*, *The Vicar of Bray*, *The Song of the Western Men*, *All Through the Night*, *The Carrion Crow*. I cannot erase the worst hymn: 'New every morning is the love, our wakening and uprising prove.' We danced around a maypole. We took bus trips to singing competitions and, the best part, ate picnic lunches. In the church choir, I earned one shilling and sixpence for a wedding and threepence more for a funeral. On Sunday, I folded *The Hotspur* into my cassock to see me through the sermon. After choir practice in winter, I hurried home, afraid of the dark, as the trees hissed and thrashed like witches. At Wolf Cub evenings, we wore caps and green jumpers and slithered like snakes in the long grass, concealed from the enemy. In the Scout hall, we sat with Akela around a makeshift camp fire, a dim light bulb cloaked in red crêpe paper.

Two hours of bliss filled our Saturday mornings at the Regal. We discovered what happened to the hero of the serial who last week had been dangling inches above the snapping crocodiles. We saw Hopalong Cassidy or Gene Autry or Roy Rogers, Tarzan, cartoons, the Three Stooges and Laurel and Hardy. There was always a groan when the film broke and had to be mended. In the interval, there was ice cream and a prize draw. The cinema manager wore a moustache and a bow tie. It was that posh.

★

Dad worked the summer through, called the last tombola, detonated the last hokey-cokey, sang the final *Floral Dance* and then, mercifully, the last camp anthem, which included the line: 'We laugh and smile at everything.' One September, when the last holidaymakers had departed, Dad finally trapped the office rat in a cage. We boys followed wide-eyed as he headed for the swimming pool and drowned it in the azure waters.

As a free man, he led us on family blackberrying forays and supported the Portsmouth football team. My sister arranged her marriage date and Dad reached for his pocket fixture list. Portsmouth were playing at home that day. 'You'll have to choose another date,' he said. After a match, he liked an hour in a street market, and, to Mum's dread, always brought something home. I remember an antique wind-up gramophone and a selection of 78 rpm records, including Charles Trenct's *La Mer*, which we wore out. One Saturday Dad reached conjuror-like into his coat and extracted a small, white dog he called Charlotte.

My father led our platoon to the Regal on winter evenings. Mum avoided westerns. 'It's all horses' bottoms to me, dear,' she said. If she were not with us, Dad filled the short walk with his history of the Royal Marines, including the capture of Gibraltar and the treaty of Utrecht, or his marksman's lecture concerning breath control while squeezing the Lee-Enfield trigger. The films ran in a loop: main feature, B-film and newsreels, and, like most people, Dad went in as soon as he had paid. We might see big time stuff: John Wayne, his Colt blazing in the showdown. We watched everything until we caught up and Dad said: 'This is where we came in.' If there were a John Wayne shoot-out, however, we always watched it again. The first film I saw with Mum and Dad was called, unforgettably, *Blood on the Moon*. I was aged seven or eight.

The projector beam cut through a fog of tobacco smoke. Dad detested smoking, but liked a pinch of snuff. He let me try it once and laughed at my streaming tears. I never heard my father swear. He occasionally referred to someone as 'a BF', but always added: 'Pardon my French.' We liked his service slang. He never described a man as drunk. He always said he was 'three quarters shot away'.

Sometimes Dad took us to Portsmouth and to the sergeants' mess in the Royal Marines barracks. We breathed aromas of polish, tobacco and beer. A brass cannon gleamed in the foyer, a dumb waiter squeaked and snooker balls clicked. Lemonade for us, a pint for Dad, a small stout for Mum. Dad enjoyed the gossip of his old friends. In time he went less frequently, then kept up with events as a subscriber to the corps magazine, *The Globe and Laurel*. He wore a Royal Marines tie almost every day and gave me one. I have it still, never worn.

The horrible day of the eleven-plus results mingled relief and disappointment. Friendships crumbled, we went our separate ways. I made the rail journey to Churcher's college at Petersfield. Its clock tower suggested the frontispiece of a school novel. The school anthem had an Etonian flourish: '*Credita Caelo*, lustily we sing, *Floreat Churcheria*, let the rafters ring.' As a grammar school under the 1944 Education Act, it housed two tribes, boarders and day boys. Boarders were already embedded. They smelled slightly of the laundry and walked around shaking bottles of milk to make a crude butter. Their custom was to settle quarrels with fist fights behind the swimming pool. Greedy senior boys doled out lunch, short rations at long tables. At Churcher's I started to learn Latin and played rugby. I won the junior cross-country. My only crime, 'Chattering like a parrot,' was punished by an hour's detention. Thirty years later I boarded a plane in Paris and the man who took the seat next to mine remembered me. 'We were in the same class at Churcher's,' he said. 'I recognize you by your teeth.'

I had been two terms at Churcher's when Dad's dream of running a pub came true. I went to a school in Portsmouth. The pub was at the gates of Portsmouth football ground. Crowds shouted: 'Good Old Monty,' when Lord Montgomery, the club's president, came to matches. Dad took me to games and I felt his disappointment when I showed no appetite for football. The terraces reeked of beer and bladders. Spectators who felt faint were passed over the heads of the crowd to ambulance men below. I used to see some of Portsmouth's football stars sitting in Dad's pub after training sessions, relaxing with cigarettes and pints.

Dad's famous football story started with Portsmouth winning the FA Cup in 1939. The cup was kept in a Portsmouth bank vault through the war and was sometimes displayed at supporters' gatherings. One evening Dad was chosen to guard it during the night. He slid the crown jewel of English football under his bed and tethered it with string to his big toe. I asked Mum if this were true. 'That,' she replied firmly, 'is what your father always said.'

★

School lunch at the Portsmouth Southern grammar school was better ordered than feeding time at Churcher's. Masters sat at tables. One of them urged us to follow his example and chew each mouthful thirty-two times. Such thorough mastication, however, did not stop him talking. Wise boys took shelter at the end of the table. Two of my classmates created an admirable yellow cloud in the chemistry laboratory, an exploit for which the entire class of thirty was caned by an enthusiastic deputy head, a lesson to the innocent that life is unfair. The headmaster at the time was said to dislike the Portsmouth accent but did not cane in pursuit of better diction. There were plenty of other whacking offences. We wondered where schoolmasters learned how to do it.

I enjoyed English and French and with a passable Franglais played Princess Katherine in *Henry V.* I joined the cadet force and wore a uniform once a week, a naval rating's rig. I pressed the seven concertina creases of the bell-bottom trousers, slipped on a blue collar, wriggled into the top, put on my cap, blancoed belt and gaiters and buffed my boots. I learned to fire a Lee-Enfield and remembered Dad's lecture on caressing the trigger. I went on a course at a naval air station and flew for the first time, a thrilling experience. The aircraft was a biplane Dragon Rapide.

By now I was a veteran long-distance cyclist. With friends, I rode to Land's End and Stratford-upon-Avon. I cycled to Hereford to see my grandmother. She showed me a framed photograph of my grandfather on the wall. Whenever the talk turned to the great war, she always wept and said: 'All those lovely Welsh boys.'

Dad put theatre and cinema posters in the bar and in exchange received free tickets. I squired my mother to films, plays and variety shows. As head of holidays she packed picnics and took us on coach trips to Cheddar caves, the Isle of Wight, seaside towns, the New Forest and Stonehenge where we enjoyed scrambling on the great stones, a pleasure not available today. Dad rarely took a holiday, but he sometimes hired a taxi and took us all to see his family in Hereford. He disliked London, but showed me the sights there once for my education's sake. I described our day to Mum and said Dad and I had eaten 'chestnuts roasted on a red-hot brazier'. Since I pronounced it 'brassiere' I hear their merry laughter still.

I often swam at Southsea beach from a slope of shingle and sand known as the Snake Pit. From this place, as long as I could remember, I had watched the liners in their majesty, *Queen Elizabeth*, *Queen Mary*, *United States* and others, rounding the eastern end of the Isle of Wight and turning for the Channel. At teatime on Thursdays Union Castle liners departed Southampton for Cape Town. Since I was a small boy I watched aircraft carriers, battleships, cruisers, destroyers, frigates, minesweepers and submarines, entering and leaving Portsmouth. I liked their names: *Formidable*, *Illustrious*, *Implacable*, *Intrepid*, *Invincible*, *Indefatigable* and *Indomitable*, and I fancy that the navy taught me to spell. Spithead, the Solent and Portsmouth harbour were busy with ferries and working boats. The Portsmouth of my boyhood had been a naval headquarters for five centuries.

Behind the dockyard's high walls worked thousands of shipwrights, artificers, electrical engineers and others. They arrived each morning as a tinkling bicycle swarm beneath a moving cloud of tobacco smoke. In the evening the same thousands put on their cycle clips, lit up and set off, pedalling north, past the house where Charles Dickens was born in 1812. What words he could have written about the bicycle armada.

★

I whittled at notions of what I might do in the afterlife, the years beyond school. Before I was fourteen, I imagined myself an adventurer in the mystery of newspapers, a reporter. I was devoted to the papers. I knew the names of foreign correspondents like René MacColl, Ralph Izzard, David Holden, Noel Barber, James Cameron, Donald Wise. I even read my father's copy of *The Morning Advertiser*, the organ of the licensed trade. By now my mother and father had moved to another pub on the edge of Portsmouth.

A terse advertisement in the Portsmouth *Evening News* flagged me down: 'Wanted for this newspaper, junior reporter.' I saw it as a Kitchener's finger, pointing at me, and I wrote at once. After an interview, the paper offered me a job, depending on my performance in the recent summer exams. When the results arrived, I set my compass.

I saw the headmaster. He said that journalism was not a proper job. Dad, too, pursed his lips. He had hoped I would go for something safe. Still, seeing that my mind was made up, he knew what to do. He took me at once to Burton's. I chose a light grey suit. He selected a more practical blue one, so thick it looked bulletproof. To this he added two white shirts and a maroon tie.

I had several times read *My Turn to Make the Tea,* Monica Dickens's novel of local newspaper life. Her heroine had been sacked and replaced by 'a lad of sixteen fresh from school'. I was sixteen. I was that boy. Instead of being a teenager, I would be a junior reporter.

On the last day of September 1957, I wore the blue suit. Dad presented me with a pen as a kind of baton, then I was on my own. Ascending the curving stairs at the *Evening News*, I was aware of a deliciously bracing smell of printers' ink and hot metal. This was surely the cordite of news. I took a baptismal sniff and pushed the heavy black door of the reporters' room.

Chapter 3

Kicking the kettle

I expected to hear telephones shrilling and newshounds barking. I imagined shirtsleeves and a cigarette haze, just as I had seen on the cinema screen. At this early hour, however, the news tide was at slack water, the newsroom almost bare, telephones mute. Mr Wilkinson, the dapper news editor, devotedly scissored cuttings from newspapers, primping them into little stacks as trim as his grey moustache.

He opened the big desk diary and the list of assignments of the day. It was the first time I had seen my name preceded by Mr. My lowly task was to compile a list of programmes from the *Radio Times*, a chore as dull as picking oakum, but intended to teach typing. Wilkie, as I learned to refer to him, showed me how to place a carbon between two sheets of copy paper. I pecked at the keys like a damaged crow.

What happened next was theatre. Enter, stage right, journalists. The newsroom door banged open. A tumble of reporters blew in, throwing off jackets and yacking and phoning, cig packets open in ammo box style.

At the back of the room a feature writer settled into his own adjectival world, peacefully pasting cuttings into a book, dreamily stirring his tea with the glue brush.

The copy flowed in, an unstoppable stream. Copy-tasters winnowed the wheat. Dud copy died on the spike like the victims of Vlad. Sub-editors administered first aid to grammar and tailored the headlines. The sports editor wheeled out his Capstan Full Strength. Stories queued on chattering teleprinters. Some stuff came handwritten. Some came typed with such violence that the letter O perforated the paper.

From puddled telephone boxes reporters dictated their copy to a small corps of typists at head office.

'Thanks, sweetie,' they concluded, 'toodle-oo.'

The sweeties said 'toodle-oo', too.

They rolled up the dictated words, popped them into arterial pneumatic tubes and sent them whizzing to the sub-editors' room. The main front page story was agreed and set up. In the inky-apron zone typesetters' fingers turned lead into language. Photographs flowed in. Overnight crime, car crashes, city council schemes, naval news, court cases and just-fancy-that filled the columns. The women's page, theatre reviews, the pop music column, sports news and crossword fell into place.

So did Letters to the Editor: 'Sir, Am I the only reader to notice the decline in manners?'

Printers bolted curved steel plates to the rollers. Presses roared. The whole printing house trembled. Thrilled to be even the merest minuscule in this thundering purpose, I was determined to be a useful apprentice. Over the months, I learned shorthand at two-hour evening classes, my speed improved by digestive biscuits and coffee brought at half-time by the teacher's daughter.

On the press benches of the magistrates' courts, old hands showed me the law in action and how to report it. Some of them were still in their thirties; some had been in bombers or the army or the navy. Learning press bench reporting was like learning to fly sitting next to the pilot.

Courts dealt in misfortune, greed, cruelty, foolishness, violence, weakness, cunning, sadness, love, truth and lies. In the coroner's court, I wrote of accidents, abortion and suicide. The juvenile court was a place of troubled beginnings. My first experience in the courts lasted six months. Sometimes shoplifters and others slipped notes to reporters, pleading: 'For my family's sake please keep my name out of the paper.'

'It all goes in the paper,' said Wilkie. He showed his own steely way with crime by cutting a penny from my expenses claim for a tenpenny bus fare. On Friday morning, I collected my weekly pay of £2 5s, and on Friday afternoon went with other junior reporters to classes in press law, discussions of new books and critiques of our essays.

Wilkie always had work for me. He sent me to interview the Portsmouth gunner who fired the first shell at Jutland in 1915. 'People like other people's stories,' he said. 'This is a navy city. We want to hear the roar of the gun.' Sending me to a golden wedding couple, he said:

'Come back with a story. Ask them the secret of marital bliss, make us smile.' He dispatched me to the railway station to meet a Portsmouth man visiting home after forty years in America. The story was worth a picture. Dave, the photographer, carried a big Micro-Press camera. Fearing that we might miss our man, I asked Dave how we would recognize him in the crowd pouring from the London train. 'He'll be wearing a big American hat,' Dave said confidently, 'they always do.' A Stetson bobbed in the distance. God bless America. We headed towards it.

A reporter introduced me to the office pub. Noting my callowness, the barmaid said: 'Half a pint for him then.'

In a city like Portsmouth, reporters needed to speak some navy, to know an officer's rank by his gold sleeve rings and a rating's job by his arm badge; to remember that a submarine was a boat, not a ship; the difference between mooring and berthing; and not to call a frigate a destroyer.

Sub-editors wrinkled their noses at careless grammar, cut out words like brainchild and comfy, banned by the paper, and were merciless with hackneyed phrases.

'You've written that the council agreed spending to the tune of £5,000. How does that tune go?'

'You say that during her visit the Queen showed no sign of her recent cold. What did you expect her to do? Spit out of the window?'

A sub kindly watered the purple in my account of a trip in a Trinity House ship relieving lightships in a Channel gale. "Thank God you're safe,' he said, 'we thought it was world war three.' I valued the advice of a sub-editor who wanted to say: 'Keep it short' or 'Keep it taut' and conflated the two with 'Keep it tert.'

Still, even sub-editors faltered. A headline, *Queen's success at Petworth Show, first prize for Windsor cow*, was never forgotten.

After a year at head office, young reporters went to work in an outpost with a senior hand. I joined Reg Betts, a wartime bomber veteran whose moustache curled as jauntily as his pipe. He commanded a swathe of Hampshire, wore check shirts and tweed and loved reporting. He cut a figure in the town, his progress marked by chats with policemen, councillors, clergymen and undertakers.

'Nothing of interest this week, Mr Betts,' a funeral director said, 'but a cold snap's coming.'

Reg taught me to ride the office motorbike and sent me questing among the villages, to take the rural pulse and harvest the stories and fill the columns. I called at a rectory. A figure in the creaking doorway appeared as bleak as an Easter Island statue. There was no news. He croaked these words every week. An elderly clergyman said that a conference of rural deans was beyond anyone's understanding. He dictated fifty words of explanation: far more, he said, than churchgoers would want to read even if they could understand. I wrote up the parish council arguments and described the annual ritual of a horse entering a pub to drink a pint of beer. Reg never accepted the excuse that there was no news. There was always news, he said. You just had to dig.

Wilkie came to inspect Reg's domain and joined our regular morning meeting in a nearby café. He went out and returned to the office with a kettle he had just bought. He advised Reg that coffee could more efficiently be made in the office. He wished us good day and left. I saw a wicked gleam in Reg's eye. He placed the kettle on the floor and kicked it across the room. It hit the wall with a glorious clatter of defiance. It was never used. Coffee was forever in the café.

Reg took me to a pub to meet some of his Fleet Street friends who were working on a story about runaway lovers. The girl's father said he would speak to only one reporter. Fleet Street's finest had to choose. In the pub's small saloon bar, the tables were pushed back. Reg and I watched as the *Daily Herald* and the *Sunday Pictorial* stripped to the waist and wrestled for the interview.

I graduated from the magistrates' courts to the quarter sessions and the assize court at Winchester where the judge sat beneath a version of King Arthur's round table. As juries pondered, veteran policemen and reporters, men of much the same mind, smoked and reminisced, noting that murder trials had lost their edge since hanging ended.

The traditions of naval courts martial never failed to impress. Feet were stamped and the accused officer's sword lay on a table through his trial, the point of the blade turned towards him if he were found guilty.

I became a reporter of everything: of trials, of murders, fires, strikes, robberies, crashes, warship homecomings, council meetings, farmers' meetings, union meetings, funerals, films and plays and the dreaded evening dinners that reporters called gutdowns. At twenty I had heard every after-dinner joke. I enjoyed writing about cricket, but disliked the penitential football matches played in mud. I never had my eyes open when a goal was scored. Of course I had a ringside seat at boxing tournaments. A heavyweight landed on my notebook and showered me with blood.

I first tasted lobster and champagne at a ship-launching lunch at Cowes. Vessels slid into the Medina river in an uproar of rusty drag chains. I wrote up the social event of the Cowes year, the August regatta, where the Royal family came to sail and glowering old naval men encrusted the yacht club balconies like molluscs. Uffa Fox was the celebrated chief citizen, yacht designer and sailing companion to the Duke of Edinburgh. As breezy as Cowes itself, and totally discreet about princes, he always helped me with a few sentences about boats and sailing. 'Now don't you go putting all that in your paper, my boy,' he said cheerfully. At Cowes I interviewed Alan Villiers, the Australian adventurer who sailed, owned and filmed the last of the Cape Horn clippers. I learned to sail near Cowes. The pleasure endured. The island bred adventure at a time when men and women took to the oceans in small sailing boats. Few made it beyond the Azores. In 1962 I interviewed the disarmingly modest couple, Eric and Susan Hiscock, on their return to Yarmouth from their second circumnavigation in *Wanderer III*. They had carved an Arthur Ransome phrase on their companionway. 'Grab a chance,' it said, 'and you won't be sorry for a might-have-been.' These words stayed with me, like Eric Hiscock's description in 1959 of the seas of the Southern Ocean. 'Probably the heaviest in the world, and only a very brave man with the springs of adventure strong in him would venture to take a small vessel there.' When I boarded *Wanderer III*, Eric was furiously typing an article, a man oppressed by a deadline. Susan did much of the talking and smiling. I was happy just to be sitting in their saloon.

In my nylon shirt period, I lived in digs. The landlady's cigarettes had etched a tar stain from her lip to her nostril. 'Go easy on the jam,' she said, 'it's all we have to the end of the week.' I left my bedroom tap running one day and the flood brought down the plaster of the ceiling below. I did it a second time and had to leave for new digs. A doctor called when I was ill and sat on my bed brushing away the ash falling from his cigarette onto my chest. 'Tonsillitis,' he diagnosed, 'so no smoking for you, my boy.' In the bitter winter, I ingeniously heated the lid of a biscuit tin to make a fine bedwarmer. But I overdid the heating and it burned a black square in the bed. I had to move.

An escape by prisoners from the Isle of Wight's jails always enlivened things. Fleet Street and top detectives arrived theatrically in speedboats from Southampton, wearing hats and belted mackintoshes. The papers published pictures of the prison with the escape route shown by a white dotted line. Policemen had a break from routine and the papers had headlines. Bedraggled and hungry, the fugitives were soon in the bag again.

I left the *Evening News* and worked for news agencies supplying stories to Fleet Street. On the day President Kennedy was assassinated in Dallas in 1963, I made a routine call to the office in Bournemouth. 'We're all sitting here,' said the boss, 'trying to find the Bournemouth angle.'

Dennis Stevens, editor of *Hampshire*, a glossy illustrated magazine, encouraged me to write pieces for him. One was a detailed account of Lord Montagu's battle against death duties, and his pioneering transformation of his stately home at Beaulieu into a money earner complete with a motor museum. For the first time my name was on my writing; and I wrote often. Another of *Hampshire*'s regular writers was John Arlott. Dennis introduced me to him over dinner in an Italian restaurant in Southampton, and John introduced me to wine, relating how he had developed his taste for it in 1949. He smoked Passing Clouds cigarettes. He also made television ads for pipe tobacco: 'You're bound to like St Bruno, it's the most regular flake of all.'

I met him at cricket matches in Portsmouth where he combined radio commentary for the BBC with writing for *The Observer*. He compiled his *Observer* essays with a fountain pen on foolscap sheets. In his final editing, he circled words and sentences and directed them elsewhere with long arrows, giving his copy a snakes and ladders appearance. It was a chore for him, however, to file his piece by phone. He paid me ten shillings to do it, enough for two suppers in those days. Reading his narrative of the day's play was itself an education. I knew John's son, James, a reporter on the *Echo* in Southampton. On the last day of 1964, I was with James at a friend's new year party in Southampton. James took his girlfriend home and was afterwards killed when he drove his car into the back of a lorry. He was twenty years old.

I saw John from time to time, mostly at cricket grounds. I also met him by chance in the Isles of Scilly. He invited me to dinner. I went to buy wine in a hotel. There had been a run on it, the landlord said, only one bottle of Mouton Cadet remained. I bought it and gave it to John. He showed it to Valerie, his wife, and said: 'Look at this lovely wine. We'll drink it at once.' As we sipped I noticed a dozen or so Mouton Cadet on the sideboard, John's haul from the hotel.

Leslie Thomas, a journalist on the London *Evening News*, told me about his enjoyable job, writing features. 'You should try to get into this kind of work. It's a great life.' I was married and lived in Portsmouth. Leslie's enthusiasm made me think deeply about going to Fleet Street. He urged me to give it a go. He himself wrote *The Virgin Soldiers* in 1966, the first of his bestsellers.

My Fleet Street ambition pushed me. I thought I might have a chance at *The Times*. Under the editorship of William Rees-Mogg, it was looking for reporters to modernize its coverage. John Grant, the managing editor, interviewed me. He was encouraging. I took some of my bylined articles. Rees-Mogg had introduced bylines in 1967, saying that they improved the quality of writing. 'For a journalist,' he argued, 'his name is his career.' John Grant wrote to me saying I could start as one of the 'taxi rank' of reporters ready to tackle any job, or I could have 'an independent command in Wales'. I liked the sound of that and said so.

Julian Mounter, my predecessor, insisted on showing me the territory in Wales and Bristol, then drove us to Dartmoor and on to Cornwall. The whole west of England was part of my diocese. We interviewed Daphne du Maurier. She poured tea and sliced the cake. She was rather striking. The belt cinched over her pink jumper gave her the look of an exotic Akela. On the edge of my new job a Cornish tea with Daphne du Maurier seemed a perfect start.

Chapter 4

Stinging nettle soup

Sometimes, in the hinterlands of Wales, *The Times* itself seemed as rare as a unicorn. I once asked for a copy of it in a shop among the hills. This was somewhere on the woodsmoke line, that mysterious Welsh latitude of fragrant chimneys.

'Oh dear,' the shop assistant said, 'we've only one copy left and that's the doctor's.'

She was, however, a kindly star, and resourceful. She smiled and took me to a chair and placed *The Times* in my hands.

'Now you sit here, love, and you read it, and when you've finished I'll iron it for the doctor.'

And so I did, and so did she. Dashing away with the smoothing iron, she made *The Times* pristine for medical fingers.

I started writing from Wales in December 1968. I was a clean skin. I had never seen Cardiff or a colliery, a steelworks or Snowdon. In a pub whose name I could not utter, I feared that tongue surgery might be the only way forward. Wales, however, was my chosen canvas and the assignment embraceable. Mine was the unfolding story of a people and their country in dramatic times, history on the anvil.

Fortunately for me, history was being unearthed in Wales on a grand scale. Pioneer professors had moved on from medieval and Tudor times to modern social history, the lives of the people, the new discovery of Wales.

Wynford Vaughan-Thomas, historian and journalist, who knew every cwm and summit, was encouraging. 'Wales,' he pointed out, 'is a country of just the right size for one person to know well in one lifetime.' Somehow its 8,000 square miles has become an international unit of area.

Wales was welcoming, too. A headmaster invited me to present prizes at his school's speech day and, over lunch, gave me the afternoon's programme. Seeing the letters MA tacked to my name, I said I had no such honour. 'Don't give it a thought,' said the head, 'in Wales, we are all MAs.'

To start writing, one must start writing. For a reporter, nothing beats going and seeing. I asked for a trip underground. The cage descended 400 yards. The walk to the coalface was long. The miners talked of the only job they knew. In the years since 1958, the coal board in Wales had axed 50,000 Welsh jobs. In 1969 I wrote from Blaengwynfi in Glamorgan: 'At dawn on Saturday the nightshift men will be lifted to the surface at the colliery here for the last time and the pit will close. For many young men in south Wales, it will re-emphasize the writing on the wall: for them there can be no future in mining.'

In coal and steel, a way of life was shrinking before our eyes.

Argument, I was told, was a Welsh tradition. I have been able to find only one village in the world called Loggerheads, and it is in Wales. Thomas Jones, Lloyd George's civil servant confidant, once sketched his countrymen as 'intemperate and inflammable, but neither cruel nor murderous, and slanderous within the bounds of the law'.

In 1969 a Welsh clamour was rattling the cutlery in London. It derived from crisis in coal, steel, language and rural life. Uncertainty prevailed. Into this drama in the spring of 1969 stepped the Prince of Wales, twenty years old and anxious to please. Nine weeks ahead of his investiture at Caernarfon, he drove to the university in Aberystwyth to immerse himself in Welsh language and history. I saw him arrive in his green Rover as a crowd cheered. He enrolled in the college as Windsor C. A college cleaner kindly offered him help with his vowels. George Thomas, the acid drop secretary of state for Wales, feared that behind college walls Charles might be brainwashed by nationalists. He urged the prime minister to warn the Queen.

The point of Aberystwyth was that Charles should learn more about the culture of Wales than any of his forerunners, an easy ambition to achieve. In time the tutor reported that Windsor C 'shows promise'. The prince made a speech in modest Welsh and called for tolerance. Aberystwyth was a success, and so, mostly, was Caernarfon, a Welsh television spectacle seen worldwide. Charles toured Wales and harvested applause wherever he went. 'Enillodd y dydd,' a spectator concluded, 'he has won the day.' It was hard to imagine, however, that there would ever be another pageant like it.

The investiture held a mirror to tensions in Wales. The Welsh Language Society conducted a campaign of civil disobedience. Activists were jailed and fined, and some magistrates were moved to pay the fines. The cultural blood pressure could be measured in the courts. The campaign led to improvements in Welsh education and legal rights; and the sensible and practical remedy of bilingual signs on the roads and, later, in the shops.

The 1970s unfolded as a turbulent decade of strikes, elections, states of emergency, a winter of discontent, with Britain described as a sinking *Titanic*. It was a productive time to be an impartial reporter.

I had an evocative framed photograph of mountain mist and rocks, the work of a photographer of *The Times*. It was titled 'The Stones of Snowdon,' from a line in Charles Kingsley's merry invitation to Thomas Hughes, tempting him to some Welsh wandering in 1856:

> Leave to Robert Browning
> Beggars, fleas, and vines;
> Leave to mournful Ruskin
> Popish Apennines,
> Dirty Stones of Venice
> And his Gas-lamps Seven –
> We've the stones of Snowdon
> And the lamps of heaven.

The photograph inspired me to seek adventure in the mountains. Quarrying the land for an article, I spent nine days on foot, on horseback and on a railway seat from the Rhondda to Caernarfon. I blazed my trail over the Brecon Beacons, followed the spouting waterfalls, crossed Epynt with permission, walked the road the soldiers called Piccadilly and reached Llanwrtyd Wells. I started for Tregaron next day, riding half the journey through the Irfon Valley on a mountain pony with a companionable local butcher as guide. 'Pony trekking is good tourism,' he said. 'Farmers hire ponies, guesthouses have beds and I provide food.'

I exchanged the pony for Shanks's and arrived sodden at the Talbot Inn to wring out my hat and stay the night. In sunshine, and astride another pony, I rode with a farmer. 'A man needs three or four dogs to work sheep,' he said. 'I train them for two years and they work five years before they are worn out.'

We rode to the abbey ruins at Strata Florida and parted in the mountains. I walked to the inn at Ponterwyd where George Borrow stayed during his epic walk through Wales in 1854. I had his entertaining *Wild Wales* for company. Borrow was large, a man for taverns and mountain paths. He once wangled whisky from a temperance inn. He listened well and coaxed stories from people. If they spoke only Welsh, well, he had learned some from a Welsh groom in Norwich. He walked from Chester to Holyhead, to Bala, to Tregaron and Swansea. At Chepstow, his last stop, he heroically drank water from the Wye, ate dinner with a bottle of red wine, then bought a first-class ticket on the London train.

From Ponterwyd, I crossed Plynlimon wilderness, where Wye and Severn rise, to stay at Machynlleth. A train ate up some of the coastal miles, then I walked the long way to Caernarfon and dipped my feet in the Menai Strait.

'Walked far?' a fisherman asked.

'From the Rhondda.'

He cast his line and nodded: 'It's been done before, I expect.'

★

The Times liked to publish short essays, snapshots of constituencies and personalities in the run up to general elections. Montgomery, I wrote, was made of small farms, sheep, verdant valleys, black and white timbered houses and benign mountains. Liberals held the political reins. It was rumoured that when Mr Emlyn Hooson, QC, was re-elected in 1970, people knelt as he passed through a village. As a farmer, he understood sheep-raising country. As a Welsh speaker, he ensured, even in London, that his children had a bilingual education. Of his election opponents, the Conservative was the strongest runner. This was Mr William Williams Wynne, a dashing subaltern of a candidate. His slogan 'William Williams Wynne Will Win,' sounded like a tongue-twister in a police sobriety test. He called himself 'an outspoken chap', and said his privileged background, which included Eton, was a disadvantage. 'People prefer a self-made man to a ready-made one, but I'm going to work and work till I get in. I have already flogged myself to death.'

The headline on my story was: 'Will Mr William Williams Wynne Win?' The electorate's answer was no.

★

Before I knew what a philosopher was, I grew up with newspaper images of Bertrand Russell, a man thin and beaky with a bush of white hair. Once, during his Campaign for Nuclear Disarmament days in the 1960s, he seemed to have gone to earth. Through a friendly tip-off, I found him in a small hotel in the Isle of Wight and he invited me to tea on the terrace. Tea, I later discovered, was a passion with him, particularly a fragrant China brew he described as 'half aromatic, half like meadows in June'. Conversation was another passion. He said it was wonderful that through one intermediary you could vault the years. His grandfather, Lord John Russell, had conversed with Napoleon in Elba in 1814 and had described the event to young Bertie in the 1870s. And here on the hotel terrace was old Bertie telling me.

Bertrand Russell lived for half a century at Plas Penrhyn in north Wales, his anchorage between gaunt mountains and the sea. From this peaceful place, during the Cuban missile crisis, he sent telegrams to Kennedy and Khrushchev. His habit was to sip a large measure of Red Hackle whisky in his bedroom and watch the sun sink over Tremadog Bay. He was ninety-seven when he died at eight o'clock in the evening of 2 February 1970. The night desk of *The Times* telephoned me. I left Cardiff at three in the morning and drove for five hours to interview Russell's neighbours and friends. At Plas Penrhyn, one of Russell's staff showed me the Red Hackle bottle from which the philosopher had poured his last drink. American admirers once wrote to the distillers saying that Red Hackle clearly did not diminish Russell's 'mental or sexual power', and asked if anything like it was made in America.

35

A few days later, I watched the humblest of hearses arrive with the plainest of coffins at Colwyn Bay crematorium. The Russell family paid brief homage. 'Bertrand Russell resisted the parsons all his life,' I was told. In his departure there was no ceremony: no words, no music, no crowd.

Bertrand Russell's neighbours included Clough and Amabel Williams-Ellis. Clough started building his theatrical village of Portmeirion in 1925, setting it on a hillside above the entrancing Dwyryd estuary. Clough was a tall stick and wore a tweed jacket, a bow tie, knee breeches and yellow stockings. He traced his ancestry to a Welsh prince of the twelfth century. He remembered Queen Victoria's jubilee of 1887, saw his first car in 1895, met W G Grace, danced at a ball where candlewax dripped romantically from the chandeliers onto his shoulders. He and Amabel, a sister of Lytton Strachey, invited me to lunch at their seventeenth-century home, Plas Brondanw, near Portmeirion. Amabel had been out foraging, so we had her delicious and special stinging nettle soup with cheese. Clough was ninety. Amabel, who was eighty, said that during her recent trip to Katmandu, she had had difficulty adopting the cross-legged lotus position.

Portmeirion grew in Clough's boyhood imaginings as a whimsical home for arches, belvederes, colonnades, cobbles, cottages, urns, façades, fountains, a campanile, of course, and pink and primrose houses among cypresses, azaleas and rhododendrons. He awarded plaques to fine summers; one of them: 'To the summer of 1959 in honour of its splendour.'

'Portmeirion,' Clough explained, 'is unashamedly romantic and expresses what I feel. It shows that we can develop beautiful landscape without defiling it. I felt a sadness that so many people were missing so much. I wanted them to find architecture entertaining. Critics say I'm an old romantic and anti-modernist, but even moderns of the most severe rectitude come to Portmeirion for a good wallow. I have tried to persuade my brethren that men are not machines, but soft and tender animals. Portmeirion shows that architectural good manners can be good business. I fight for beauty.'

Clough and Amabel showed me Plas Brondanw and its garden. They served tea before a log fire, then took me to a desk set with a typewriter and paper. They invited me to write, and so I did. How could I not?

★

For a while I collected the nicknames of Wales because they were vanishing so rapidly and deserved to have their story told.

Dai Bread and Jones the Milk were dropping out of the vernacular. So was Emlyn Kremlin, the communist, and Dai-Up-and-Down with the gammy leg. Who now remembers that Sir David Maxwell Fyfe, the home secretary, was ever Dai Bananas in Wales? Who recalls that Dai Drop was a paratrooper, that Harry Greensuit and Jones Spats paid a lifelong price for their fashion errors, that Dai Quiet Wedding, being poor, married in plimsolls?

Such names enriched Welsh life for more than a century, useful in crowded valleys where the paucity of surnames created confusion of identity. Most Welsh surnames derive from forenames: Davies, Edwards, Thomas, Hughes, Evans, Roberts, Griffiths, Williams and Lewis. Jones grew from John. In 1853, a Registrar General's report noted: 'The name of John Jones is in Wales a perpetual incognito.' The numerous Joneses appearing in a court case in 1894 created a 'patronymical bedlam'. People therefore avoided confusion by adding an identifier: Jones the Post, Jones the Meat and Jones the Stitch, who was a tailor. Farmers still take the name of their farms, Jones Craig-ddu for example, and many miners took the names of their pits: Evans Deep Duffryn and Williams Navigation. Welsh soldiers still add part of their service number to their name: Sergeant Evans 123. For distinction's sake, many people sought a twig in the family tree to add a balancing decoration to Jones, creating Vaughan-Jones, or Parry-Jones, or Mars-Jones.

Nicknames became an aspect of Welsh humour. Dai Piano was not a musician, but a notorious cadger. 'No cigarettes today, Dai?' – 'No, I left them at home on the piano.' Exactly Jones was named after his favourite and most irritating word. Jones Balloon was a foreman who implored his men: 'Don't let me down, boys.' Cliff Kiosk was the Press Association reporter in Wales who seemed to live his life in a phone box.

Desmond Flower, of Cassell, the publishers, saw this essay in *The Times* and invited me to lunch in London. He was a memorable host and raconteur, but the pudding came and went and he made no mention of a book. Afterwards he helped me into my coat, and, as we shook hands, said breezily: 'You'll write a book for us, won't you?' That was it. The glow lasted all the way to Wales. It was my first book.

Richard Booth, when I first met him, was a revolutionary bookseller aged thirty. Styling himself 'King,' he transformed Hay-on-Wye into a granary of secondhand books. He had a million volumes in barns and in the castle where he lived. He collected the books himself, travelling in a chauffeured car to buy them. Being picturesque and a little remote, Hay was ideal for messing about in books. Booth gave it a modern lease of life and learning. 'I buy in bulk,' he said. 'Everyone interested in books wants second-hand ones. A Victorian volume on dentistry, for example, is almost worthless on its own, but has value alongside dozens of dentistry books. English literature has a world following and I have created a destination for browsers. All my books can be reached by someone 5ft 3in tall.'

In the world of books, these were changing times. The working-class libraries in the miners' institutes, used by self-educators like Aneurin Bevan and James Griffiths, were in decline. Everyone knew that the libraries were financed by the miners' famous pennies. But men were not reading in the same way. As pits closed in the 1960s, books gave way to slot machines and cabaret stages. Libraries were going cheap.

★

The abbot of Prinknash abbey, a Benedictine monastery in Gloucestershire, invited me to lunch. There was no conversation during the meal. The monks sat at their refectory tables and ate contemplatively while listening to one of their number reading *The Life of Nelson* by Robert Southey.

A space on the refectory wall reminded them of their turn of fortune. The painting once displayed there was sent to auction in the hope that it would raise money towards the building of a new monastery. To the monks' astonishment it raised £273,000, at that time half the cost. The new abbey is a picture of lovely honey-coloured stone and rises in a fold of the Cotswolds, near the pottery which makes Prinknash ceramics.

The abbey guestmaster showed me the library, then the lifts and showers and the centrally heated rooms for monks and ten guests. 'American monks,' he said, 'would think we are roughing it a bit without individual bathrooms, but if people believe we live a hard life in cold cells, they are mistaken. We do not have Slumberlands, but there is no point in going to absurd lengths of frugality. The disciplines of our lives stem not from physical conditions, but from daily routine and our effort to live in harmony. We are thirty-seven human beings in a small community and have to live with one another's idiosyncrasies. If we allowed annoying things to get on our nerves, life would be impossible.'

After lunch, I joined the abbot and several monks in a small room where we had coffee and a digestive interlude of gentle talk. Coffee dribbled through fine cracks in the pot and made sparkling brown bubbles. The coffee cups, too, were slightly fractured. I enjoyed the good-humoured conversation. It was a kind of blessing. With their coffee, one or two of the monks savoured a cigarette.

★

I spent several weeks with Barry John as he composed his autobiography. I did not know Barry and had never seen him play. Like everyone in Wales, I simply knew of his genius. My job was to listen to his story and help him create an authentic picture, springing to life on the page. We met at his home in Cardiff. Usually I had dinner with him and his wife, Jan, after which he and I set to work. I asked questions and made notes. Barry talked. He had the gift of humour and a tale to tell, so we often went on until midnight.

He grew up in a 'happy, noisy and united Welsh-speaking family', in a council house in Cefneithin, Carmarthenshire, the second of six children. Carwyn James, who also lived in Cefneithin, encouraged his early promise. Barry played for Llanelli and recalled the dressing room. 'It had the pleasant and familiar dirt we liked. Everything stank. Wintergreen and Vaseline seemed to ooze from walls. A fly couldn't live there.'

He made his Wales debut in December 1966 and combined with scrum-half Gareth Edwards in a great instinctive partnership. Carwyn James described their famous symbiosis: Edwards, strong, muscular, getting the ball from the scrum and whistling it to Barry John, the dreamer, the artist, the myth figure, full of Welsh guile. You need them both, he said, just as you need optimists and sceptics, artists and materialists. Barry had ten years at the top of a rugby era and quit at the age of twenty-seven. Few knew that the match against France in Cardiff in March 1972 was his last appearance. Wales beat France, Barry kicked four penalties.

'I knew I was going to miss it a lot. I had decided that rugby should not be an obsession. I worried that adulation was alienating me from the human race. I had been changed from a rugby player into a star. I craved conversation with people who didn't want to talk about rugby. Writers started calling me a legend in my own lifetime. The phrase gave me the creeps. I had no wish to be a legend. I wanted to be me.'

He felt that parents 'should encourage children gently in sport and not be disappointed if the achievement is small. Children have to be themselves, not extensions of their parents'. Barry went into journalism after his rugby career and enjoyed the Press box atmosphere. 'People ask if I would like to be sixteen or seventeen, just starting in rugby. I don't think so. Rugby is more advanced and I don't think there is the freedom I enjoyed years ago.'

★

The daily news in Wales ran from arguments over broadcasting, the Welsh language, jail sentences for protesters, coal mining and steel making, the possibility of a devolved Welsh Assembly, angry campaigning to save a large stretch of Welsh coast being turned into a gunnery range. I recorded the ending of a Labour party era in Wales, the contemporaries of Aneurin Bevan making way for young men like Neil Kinnock, aged twenty-eight.

Around this time, I met Jan Morris and we formed a friendship of enduring merriment. BBC Radio Wales invited me to interview three journalists whose work I admired. I chose John Arlott, James Cameron and Jan Morris.

I knew Wynford Vaughan-Thomas during the years he called his Welsh renaissance, when he was director of programmes at HTV. His narrative gift had made him an outstanding broadcaster. His words came in a flow, sometimes a cascade. How he despised the 'sound bite'. His words sprang from a vigorous mind.

'I had the advantage,' he said, 'of realizing that language is sacrosanct because my parents had taught us to speak properly and read well.' Religion, he noted, played no part in his upbringing. Oxford taught him to enjoy life. In his greetings and the denouements of his stories he seemed so often an exclamation mark in human form. I see him opening his door, a vision of Merlin, face pink, white hair a halo, words melodious. A joyful raconteur, he loved the ribald fun of limericks:

> In cold, damp Blaenau Ffestiniog
> Girls make love for a penny (Welsh, ceiniog). I
> know this for a fact,
> I was caught in the act
> By Lord Hailsham, then Mr Quintiniog.

I often heard him recite a favourite verse:

> Time's winged chariot, poets say,
> Warns us to love while yet we may.
> Must I not hurry all the more
> Who find it parked outside the door?
> For those who sipped love in their prime
> Must gulp it down at closing time.

He adored French wine. In an Italian restaurant in Cardiff, a waiter poured a little wine for our host, the broadcaster Emyr Daniel. Wynford said: 'It's Italian, don't taste it, just drink it!'

As a student, Emyr had a holiday job driving an ice cream van. He

REPORTER – Trevor Fishlock

appeared in court at Carmarthen for illegally sounding the chimes on a Sunday afternoon. He conducted his defence in Welsh. The chairman of the magistrates congratulated him on his eloquence. 'Nevertheless,' he said, 'we find you guilty and there has to be a fine. Will a pound be all right?'

Gwyn Erfyl, a friend of Wynford and of Emyr, was an interviewer and producer at HTV, an unusual television figure, nonconformist minister, philosopher and former conscientious objector. He was kind and perceptive. People said he became a bon viveur after his discovery of steak. He liked lobster, too. Most of all, he enjoyed a debate with his meal and wine. He told me chapel stories, but I don't think he meant me to believe that a minister so loved his cat that, when it died, he had its coat made into a Bible cover. Gwyn invited his friend, the artist Pietro Annigoni, to Wales. On the way to dinner, Gwyn found himself following a bus taking singers to a concert. He overtook the bus, flagged it down and introduced the choir to Annigoni. There and then, they assembled on the roadside grass and burst into song. Annigoni marvelled at Gwyn's angelic power to conjure a choir in the hills.

★

Saunders Lewis was both admired and hated. He fought in the first world war as an army officer, and was a playwright, poet, teacher and a founder in 1925 of Plaid Cymru. He and two others went to jail for setting fire to a bombing school in 1936. He endured social and academic ostracism. His radio lecture in 1962 inspired the Welsh language campaign and its associated civil disobedience. He had no wish to be interviewed. Eventually I went to his home and found him in his garden wearing pinstriped trousers, a black jacket and a white open-neck shirt: a small man of seventy-eight, with bright and penetrating eyes, mowing his lawn with furious energy. Although his reputation was for prickliness, he invited me in and, since it was ten o'clock in the morning, poured sherry for both of us. I got my interview. He talked at length without pause. 'No nation ever understood another nation,' he said. 'It is impossible for Englishmen to feel for Welsh tradition.'

The language campaigners, he said, were 'not fighting against England and the English, they are fighting the most unpopular battle of all: against their own people'.

★

In Aberfan, 21 October is the longest day, the anniversary of the disaster, of the deaths of 116 children and twenty-eight adults. Most of Aberfan's people did not flee the village in their grief. The slurry mountain shattered the community, but did not destroy it. People remained, to support each other through the aftermath, to persuade the government to remove remaining tips, to express themselves through the Community Association, the choir, the village magazine and chapels. The community's enduring life has been largely the work of the people themselves.

I went to Aberfan before the tenth anniversary in 1976. A man who had lost a child said: 'Don't write about tears, write about the positive, about what we have built, how we have created a real community.' Aberfan did not want people to forget, but they believed enough had been said and they wished for a day of privacy and dignity. Although the scar is plain, the community does not dwell upon the hurt. More than anything else Aberfan's tragedy made all of south Wales look with outrage at the mountains of waste that scarred their valleys. Anger powered the desire to erase the tips and black wasteland. Responding to public mood the Welsh Office established a unique department to stimulate large scale land reclamation. The tips, once black and threatening, are shaped into hills, planted with shrubs, trees and grass. They became places for schools, clinics, homes and parks in valleys made green again.

★

In 1976 I spent a couple of days with Tom Jones, a Montgomeryshire farmer of twenty-six. It was lambing time. In the hills, we found two lambs, one dead and one alive. Tom skinned the dead one with his knife and fitted the fleece like a jersey onto the living lamb. He gently pushed it towards the ewe whose lamb had died. She accepted the orphan and moved off. Tom whistled his dogs and we set off across the mountain.

Lambing was the critical time for the farm. In March and April, Tom and his brother and parents expected 1,700 lambs, and would sell 1,300 to earn more than £20,000 to pay the taxman, bank, garage, vet and suppliers. Paperwork irritated Tom. He liked the shepherd work, a fulfilling part of his crowded life. With his boarding school education and honours degree in history, his parents had hoped to see him as a college lecturer. In choosing the farm and the hills he disappointed them a little. 'There was no choice, really. I wanted to live at my roots.'

Tom had reflected on the decline of uplands communities and the erosion of the Welsh language. He believed that decay could be resisted and repaired. In three years, he and others rejuvenated their valley's life. Local halls rang to the sound of concert and choir practice. Tom became an impresario, scriptwriter and occasional comedy performer. Between the farm, rural show business and leadership of the local youth movement, he wrote prose and poems, sometimes working on a rock ledge beside a waterfall. 'Just me, the sheep, the dogs, the fox and the crows.'

His parents' farm, near Llanerfyl, was a ready-made way of life when he left the university in Aberystwyth. He worked it with his brother and a part-time farmhand. To Tom, the farm, community and Welsh were inseparable. 'I believe I hold this patch of land for Wales, responsible for protecting and bettering it, passing it on. I want to contribute to the life of my neighbourhood and to the language. Welsh is something distinctively ours. My nationalism is cultural. I believe people should care for their own corner of the world.' Tom joined the Farmers Union of Wales, rather than the NFU, of which his father and brother were members. The FUW had a distinctive Welsh outlook. 'I joined it because they were Welshmen doing something for themselves. I admired that.'

At university, he was a member of the Welsh Language Society, but not an activist. 'My family made sacrifices and expected me to work. They would have been upset to see me go to prison for demonstrating. It was a necessary struggle. In our valley, we restarted a branch of the largest youth movement in Wales, to revitalize the life of the area. Almost everyone between fourteen and thirty is connected with it. The great talent in the countryside has never been exploited properly. We are a busy branch and Welsh is not dying here. I don't want to sound self-satisfied. I want my life to be a blend of the land, hard work and contribution to a creative Welsh-speaking community. We are sowing the seeds.'

★

In 1975 I made my first trip to America. A Boeing 707, full of Welsh businessmen and women, flew to Welsh Week in New York to drum up trade and investment. I travelled with Patrick Hannan and Geraint Talfan Davies, both friends and talented journalists. The business crowd was headed by the secretary of state and supported by a thirty-strong choir to sing the Americans into submission. The captain and two cabin staff made announcements in Welsh. With the choir in full voice there was something of the bank holiday charabanc about the trip. As the plane neared New York, the passengers had a whip-round for the crew which raised £42.

The credentials of Wales were solid enough in America. According to a perfectly serviceable legend, Madog, a Welsh prince, discovered America in 1170. Of the fifty-six signatories of the Declaration of Independence, seventeen were Welsh. A noted Capone gang racketeer was a Welshman, Murray the Hump. Surprisingly, my cab driver in Manhattan knew something of Wales. When he asked me what I was doing in New York, I told him I was going to a conference on Wales. 'Wales?' he said. 'You mean the fish, or them singing bastards?'

Chapter 5

Handshake rock

A letter came in 1977, a dream in an envelope. I was awarded a travelling fellowship lasting eight months, one of eleven fellows from eleven countries who would explore the United States by air, bus, car, canoe and mule. We would talk to Americans of all stripes. We would learn America.

Our base was Macalester College in Saint Paul, the capital of Minnesota. Some Macalester students sauntered over to take a look at us. When we marvelled at the vastness of the USA, a couple of them nodded agreement. They were Minnesota-born, they said, and had yet to see the sea.

We fellows acclimatised by driving north, beyond Bob Dylan's Minnesotan birthplace on the edge of Lake Superior. We followed the Gunflint Trail and were fitted out with Canadian canoes and other kit. We paddled among islets on the silent lakes where Canada and Minnesota merge. In the last glimmer of daylight, we reached an island with a welcoming hut and a camp fire. Next day I paddled across a lake to Canada where a Mountie stamped my passport. A canoe trip was a Minnesotan rite. People here have Scandinavian roots and outdoor minds. They love canoeing, fishing and weekending in lake-shore cabins. In winter, which bites hard here, they are addicted to cross-country skiing, ice-fishing, and holing up in their little cabins.

Macalester's teachers dunked us thoroughly in American history and politics. For a short time, I wrote for *The Worthington Globe*, a bright daily newspaper in southwest Minnesota. Jim Brandenburg, who worked there on his way to becoming a photographer of international standing, showed me the prairie. He drove me to a red quartzite outcrop to see something marvellous. Five thousand years ago, a man chiselled into the rock the shallow shape of his own right hand. I could not resist sliding my own hand into it, a handshake across the centuries. Among these bare rocks, generations of Native Americans created 2,000 petroglyphs, pictures of eagles and elk, of figures carrying spears and wearing headdresses of bison horn. At first I found them hard to discern, but as I stared they emerged from the rock like images in a darkroom tray.

The last of these carvings were inscribed in the eighteenth century. Many depicted horses, part of a story both magnificent and sad. The horses brought by Spanish conquerors to America transformed the life of the Plains people. The age of the mounted Native Americans lasted three centuries. Then they would have seen an advancing plume of dust raised by settlers emerging from the east, a thin line growing into a great crowd.

Jim took me to a quartzite ridge sixty-five miles away to see an enduring mystery called the Blue Mound. A stone wall along this ridge is 1,250 feet long and straight as an arrow. It lies precisely east and west. At the spring and autumn equinoxes, you can stand and look along the wall to the east and watch the sun pierce the morning sky. It might remind you of midsummer morning at Stonehenge. It certainly reaches into the imagination. We do not know why the prairie dwellers built this sunrise wall.

In its vastness, the prairie keeps its mystery and solemnity. I stayed on a prairie farm and walked a stretch of it, but seemed to make no progress, as if it were a treadmill. James Fenimore Cooper thought the prairie was 'not unlike the ocean when its restless waters are heaving heavily'. Charles Dickens picnicked on the prairie in 1842 and noted its 'solitude and silence, lonely and wild. There it lay, a tranquil sea'.

Across the South Dakota border, beyond the rocks of the Badlands, I saw Mount Rushmore, its giant sculpted faces and the twenty-foot noses of Presidents Washington, Jefferson, Lincoln and Theodore Roosevelt. At Thunder Mountain, near the sad Sioux reservations of Wounded Knee and Pine Ridge, I heard an explosion: I had found the Polish sculptor Korczak Ziolkowksi. As a young man, he had worked on the faces of Mount Rushmore. Now he was carving a gigantic tribute figure of the Sioux warrior Crazy Horse. It would be 563 feet high. Dynamite was his chisel. I heard another thunder of an explosion. 'As you can hear,' his wife said to me, 'he's tied up at the moment.'

Ziolkowski started his epic Crazy Horse sculpture in 1948. He died in 1982 and the last time I looked his successors were still blasting and shaping it. The figure of Crazy Horse, when complete, will portray a noble rider mounted on a white horse, an outstretched arm pointing to the Black Hills of Dakota. Little is known about the life of Crazy Horse, although the myths are plentiful. He was killed in 1877. But to his beaten-down people he was always a spirit of hope and remains so. As the rock is blasted, pride gains strength among the Sioux and other people. They look forward to their hero's emergence, his god-like form set free from the mighty mountain.

The prairie ends halfway across Colorado at the Rocky Mountains. I boarded a train at Denver for Salt Lake City, a journey of 570 miles, fifteen hours and three meals. Three locomotives powered the train. In the dining car, unhurried waiters evoked the age before interstates and airliners. A cosy bar and a friendly bartender seemed made for Bogart and Bacall. The railway conquered great red and purple gorges. To my collection of township names I added Solitude and Rifle. Also Castle Gate, but only because Butch Cassidy robbed a train there in 1897 and got away with $8,000.

Mormon pioneers trekked 1,400 miles from Illinois in 1847 and built Salt Lake City beside the Wasatch mountains. Their church is immensely rich. A Mormon couple invited me to dinner, and the husband told me he was wrestling with a dilemma. People sometimes find it easier to confide in a stranger. 'It is a time of anguish,' he said, 'my wife has renounced the church.' She told me that she now felt liberated. 'Breaking with the church was the hardest thing I have ever done, but now I have a freedom of spirit I never knew before. You know, I had to make an effort to get coffee for you this evening. It is not permitted by the church and I feel very strange offering it to you. I would feel guilty if I drank it.' Her husband said: 'As for myself, I think I have been suspect in the church for some time because of my questioning attitude.'

In Houston, Texas, I watched the pioneering heart surgeon, Michael DeBakey, operate on a businessman with a clogged artery. A vein taken from the man's leg would be used to repair the damage. The heart's vermilion brilliance seemed assertive, as if anxious to get its owner working. Later, in conversation, a white-faced reporter asked Dr DeBakey what exercise might prevent heart attacks. The surgeon did not hesitate. 'Walk fast,' he said.

In our travels, we heard America talking, usually very frankly. We met policemen, surgeons, ranchers, editors, business barons, mayors, teachers, soldiers, broadcasters, black leaders, Mexicans, Native American chiefs, union bosses, space workers, politicians. We visited two prisons. In one of them, my guide was a prisoner. We were in Memphis on the anniversary of Elvis Presley's first post-death birthday. He was buried in his garden at Graceland, his home on Elvis Presley Boulevard. Inscribed on the plinth of a large, white statue was the single word Presley. Wreaths and flowers adorned the swimming pool. Newspaper reprints carried the headlines reporting his death. An attendant gave me a free copy. 'No charge for a fan from old England,' he said. 'No sir.'

We had an unpleasant meeting with David Duke, the 'grand wizard' of one of the factions of the Ku Klux Klan. He hosed us with words and said white people were the oppressed minority.

On the brink of the Grand Canyon in Arizona, a guide called Bud introduced me to Holy Smoke, my hired mule. This was a creature more substantial than I had expected and it had reassuringly large feet. Through the waggling ears of the mules, we had a view of the mile-deep chasm. 'Whatever happens,' Bud said, 'no one gets off his mule. It's dumb and dangerous. Sit straight and trust the mules. They've been doing this all their lives and they know best.'

Bud led us down the narrow track in single file. I saw my right foot apparently suspended over a dizzying drop. It took six hours to descend 5,000 feet to the canyon floor. We stayed in the bunkhouse of Phantom ranch and ate large steaks. In the morning, we mounted our mules and ascended the trail. At the top, we stiffly dismounted and looked with wonder at what we had achieved. Bud said: 'Come back one day.'

Two of us flew to Israel for a week in November to cover the Sadat-Begin summit in Jerusalem. I wrote commentaries for the *Minneapolis Tribune*. My companion was Nachman Shai, later a member of the Israel Knesset.

In San Francisco, we met Harvey Milk, one of the seven people elected to govern the city. As a gay man, he believed his honesty had helped to make homosexuality respectable in San Francisco. 'Bringing homosexuals into politics has been healthy for the community,' he said to me. 'It is ceasing to be remarkable. Some people don't like it, they are afraid and can't cope with it. And, sure, there are people who don't like me. Being in public life has its dangers. Everybody knows that. If you are in the public eye and people don't like you, they can take a shot at you. It's the sort of thing we do in America. I've no doubt someday some guy will get me. I guess it's on the cards.' He smiled.

Some time later a man with a gun entered the city hall and killed the mayor and Harvey Milk.

★

On my return to London in 1978, I married Penny Symon, a reporter on *The Times*'s parliamentary staff. I worked in the London newsroom and wrote a number of campaigning articles about the damage caused to children's brains by lead in petrol. A complacent British government report said leaded petrol was safe, an assertion that proved to be wrong. I went on assignments in America and Mexico.

At Cambridge university, I scribbled my notes as six of the notorious Great Train Robbery gang talked to undergraduates. 'Why are you here?' a student asked them. Buster Edwards said: 'Because we was asked.' Roy James said: 'We are here so that all of you without sin can cast stones at us.' It was not the robbers who glamorized crime, he said, it was the press. 'Anyway,' he added, 'we all regret what we did.' Buster Edwards piped up: 'I do not regret it, but no thief imagines that when he goes out on business he will be caught.' The hijackers were in Cambridge to publicize a book about the robbery written by Piers Paul Read. The president of the Cambridge Union said there had been criticism of the meeting between students and the train thieves. 'But in a democracy, criminals who have served their time have the right to come here and talk.'

At Minehead in November, reporting restrictions were lifted in the case of Jeremy Thorpe, the former Liberal leader and four other men, accused of conspiracy to murder. My colleague Michael Horsnell and I wrote several columns a day until *The Times* closed at the end of November in its dispute with the print unions.

★

I took Mum and Dad across the Channel and drove them to Ploegsteert. Dad had never expected to find his father's name on a monument, had never thought that he might see something of the battlefields. The three of us approached the monument and I showed Dad his father's name. Mum and I withdrew. Dad stood straight-backed, at attention. He looked for a long time before turning away. He was a man of seventy-one, also a boy of eight.

★

For some months, when the paper resumed publication in November 1979, I wrote *The Times* Diary feature, intended to be entertaining and, where possible, witty. One day I saw that *The Times* stylebook banished the use of the controversial honorific term 'Ms'. I wrote: 'That forlorn little word Ms is cast into the lexicographical outer darkness. This is a rallying point for common sense.' I was astonished by the fallout. *The Times* received more than 200 letters, mostly from the United States. Some were cries of outrage, by no means all. William Safire, White House speech writer and *The New York Times*'s grammar guru, discussed the argument in a column. He noted that his own newspaper did not use 'Ms'. He added: 'Trevor Fishlock is a name I have not made up.'

I started working on the foreign news desk. In 1980, I went to Hong Kong to report the opening of the colony's new metro. I was keen to see more of China and David Bonavia, the paper's correspondent, took me over the border on a railway trip. 'A day in China,' he said, 'is never wasted. It's a wonderful place to be a foreign correspondent.'

Landing and takeoff at the old Kai Tak airport was an aviation experience. Hauling themselves upwards, the jetliners appeared to shoulder their way through Mrs Wu's washing. Planes arriving on the finger of land in the harbour seemed to offer passengers a peep into her kitchen.

I wrote a newcomer's first impression of Hong Kong. Business was good in the snake shop. Fat snakes, poked at by discerning buyers, oozed luxuriously in cane cages, awaiting slaughter and deft skinning on a bloodied chopping board. The Chinese attach mystic qualities to certain foods, and my dinner host that night urged me to sup snake broth for its blood-warming properties. It was delicious. A conservative palate has no business in Hong Kong. Nor an inelastic mind. As on its tables, so on its streets, markets, waterways and vistas, Hong Kong is astonishing. A newcomer gets caught up in the sheer vital anthill busyness of the place, the unremitting sweat of its long opportunist fever, a diet as rich in adrenalin as it is in the cholesterol of those plump, crisp ducks. In one of the world's most crowded places, people are thigh by thigh on pavements no longer broad enough. Walking in the main trading districts is no saunter, but a push against the tide. Compared with the people of Hong Kong, sardines have it easy. Hong Kong noises are orchestrated by builders. New structures sprout like forced rhubarb to the roar of drills and the tympanic thud of pile drivers. Old China hands, last here ten years ago, gape at what has happened in the meantime.

★

Penny and I lived near her parents in London. Her stepfather, Sir Barnett Cocks, had retired in 1973, after forty-three years as a parliamentary Clerk. For twelve of those years, he held the senior post, Clerk of the House of Commons. He learned the arcane working of the House from men who had known Gladstone. In his early years, modern comforts were few. The Clerk's office had a large chamber pot bearing the monogram VR. Typists were called type writers. Barney's working clothes were a Victorian morning coat, white starched wing collar, white tie and black gown, all crowned with an itchy wig. For some time, he hoped he could persuade MPs to allow him a more comfortable, and more modern, outfit: but they, not least the Labour MPs, preferred him in traditional dress, wig and all. One of his modernizing achievements, however, was to appoint the first women Clerks in the history of the Commons. He and his family moved to a flat in the Commons and were relieved to find that Big Ben did not keep them awake. They regarded it as their grandfather clock.

Barney was quoted in the papers when he defined a committee as 'a cul-de-sac down which ideas are lured and then quietly strangled'. He recalled that the Commons librarian once complained to him that MPs were using the library scissors to trim their toenails. Asked about the long parliamentary debates, he said with a smile that he had mastered the art of sleeping with his eyes open.

His knowledge of Parliament and its MPs was encyclopedic. In retirement, he wrote a book about the building of the Palace of Westminster and called it *Mid-Victorian Masterpiece*. His sub-title was: *The story of an institution unable to put its own house in order.*

Chapter 6

The monsoon bird

In India, the rains were coming, but not yet. For the time being, the emissaries of the monsoon strode the stage in anger. Lightning ripped the skies, demonic gusts tore banyans from the earth and a wind called the loo scorched in from Rajasthan.

In London, Charles Douglas-Home, the foreign editor of *The Times,* offered me adventure irresistible. 'We'd like you to do India for us,' he said. 'Could you be there before the monsoon breaks?'

I took wing soonest.

In the small hours of the last day of May 1980, I landed in Delhi. No breeze whispered. The hammer of the heat lay in ambush. Rudyard Kipling had remembered such nights. He was sixteen years old when he started as a reporter in Lahore, a youth in a white suit spattered with ink. From his recollection of the monsoon's tormented prelude he shaped a line of a poem:

'Night falls heavy as remembered sin.'

In the streets and cafes of Delhi, small groups of men and women studied the meteorology charts in newspapers, pointing their fingers, following the monsoon's track from the Indian Ocean. Others put their faith in nature's herald and searched the trees for a glimpse of the black and white Jacobin cuckoo. It had a distinctive punky quiff. Its wailing song was the certain harbinger of the rains. It was called the monsoon bird.

Waiting for me in Delhi were some dusty books and a rusty camera, a radio that maintained radio silence, a tent, some perished waterproof trousers, three or four bullets but no gun, perhaps old war stuff. A Hindi dictionary from distant days had such phrases as: 'Are your bowels regular?' 'I had four motions,' 'A sepoy shot himself,' 'Undress me,' and 'He will be hanged tomorrow.' Most helpful was a large wall map of the Indian subcontinent, clearly the high commissioner edition. I contemplated it daily. How vast the territory looked: India, Pakistan, Nepal, Bangladesh, Sri Lanka, Afghanistan and Burma.

The significant part of my inheritance was an Ambassador saloon, the Indian copy of the 1954 Morris Oxford. Among so many black and white models, the apple green paintwork of *The Times* car turned many a head. It was said in the Ambassador's favour that it could be repaired anywhere in India by a mechanic or even a blacksmith. Mine broke down one day on the baking road from Rajasthan to Delhi. Within a few minutes a sister Ambassador came bustling to the rescue, driven by a Sikh wearing a striped cravat.

'Spot of bother?' he asked.

He lifted the bonnet and performed a small operation with his screwdriver. The engine barked loyally into life. The Sikh gave a cheery wave.

'We motorists must stick together, eh?'

Our garage owner in Delhi invited my wife to his daughter's wedding. We put our car into the garage for a routine service. The following day my wife squeezed into a car filled with women in wedding finery. As they bowled along, she realized that it was our car.

I started reporting India the day after I arrived. The big political news was Indira Gandhi's return to power, a formidable figure once more, reaffirming her family's destiny. Her father, Jawaharlal Nehru, educated at Harrow and Cambridge, became India's first prime minister in 1947. He died in 1964. Two years later, at the age of fifty, Indira became prime minister. Through her marriage to a Parsi journalist, she had gained the magical surname of Gandhi. It means grocer. It served her well. In India and abroad, many thought she was in some way related to the inspirational Mahatma Gandhi, the heroic 'great soul'.

Her father was a democrat and she an autocrat with none of his vision. 'My father was a saint,' she once said, 'but I am not.' Her popularity as prime minister reached a pinnacle in India's defeat of Pakistan's forces in 1971. It shrank in 1975 when, feeling cornered, she declared a state of emergency, suspended democracy and basic rights and jailed numerous opponents and journalists.

One of those she imprisoned was Kuldip Nayar, a distinguished reporter who was *The Times*'s stringer, or assistant correspondent. He had committed no offence. Mrs Gandhi simply hated journalists. She was flailing. She had also ordered *The Times* staff reporter out of India. William Rees-Mogg, who found Mrs Gandhi 'insufferably arrogant', succeeded in getting Kuldip Nayar out of prison. Kuldip became my friend and colleague, and, in due course, India's high commissioner in London.

Mrs Gandhi promoted the cult of herself. Her supporters chanted: 'India is Indira, Indira is India.' Her impatient and ruthless younger son Sanjay terrorized the poor with slum demolition and compulsory vasectomies. His mother lost the election of 1977 and was replaced by incompetent rulers. Now here she was, three years later, back in the prime minister's office. My first stories described her gathering the reins. Ominously, the bullying Sanjay, only thirty-three, was at her side again.

★

Early in the morning of 23 June, Sanjay Gandhi went flying in his sporty red American plane. He flew too low and crashed near his home in Delhi, killing himself and his co-pilot. India's 'man of tomorrow' was indispensable to his mother. Many feared his ruthlessness. I drove to the *Hindustan Times* office. In the newsroom pandemonium, I found the editor, Khushwant Singh, who knew Mrs Gandhi and Sanjay well. Steering me out of the clamour, he said kindly: 'I'll give you ten minutes.' He outlined Sanjay's character and ambition, and the meaning of Mrs Gandhi's loss. It was the start I needed.

At sunset next day, an immense sea of faces, hundreds of thousands of people, ringed Sanjay's pyre beside the river Jumna. His elder brother Rajiv touched the sandalwood logs with a brand. Mrs Gandhi sat close to the pyre and the light of leaping flame flickered on her face. Brahmachari, her tall, white-robed mystic, uttered prayers. He wielded much influence over the superstitious Mrs Gandhi. In the coming days, her son's ashes would be strewn in twenty places in rivers and the sea.

Rajiv was little known. An Indian Airlines pilot with an Italian wife and two children, he had no political ambition. The dynastic force, however, would swallow him and propel him into his brother's place. Everyone knew that. Rajiv knew it perfectly well. Sonia, his wife, was dismayed.

The shock of Sanjay's death receded into India's restlessness. A thousand dead were counted in the violence that tormented Assam in India's north-east. Newspapers headlined the scandal of the 'burning brides', young wives killed under the pressure of their in-laws' demands for more dowry money. Processions demonstrated against gang rapes and the physical harassment of women. Plentiful monsoon rain, meanwhile, took 400 lives, but, as a good monsoon, it also promised full granaries of wheat and rice. In that year of 1980, India's population grew to 650 million, twice what it was in 1950.

Penny and I lived near the red ramparts of the Purana Qila fortress, built by the Mughal emperor Humayun around 1540. We often walked there. Sometimes, at dusk, we heard tigers roaring in the shabby zoo nearby. We employed a cook and, with our neighbours, we shared a chowkidar, a night watchman warmed by a greatcoat and armed with a stick. In the small hours, chowkidars whistled or called softly to each other, a reassuring 'All's well.'

At daybreak, a boy delivered newspapers. In this cool hour, I read them on the veranda and absorbed the amazements of India. Mynahs nattered and strutted and shrieked like politicians. Bulbuls bustled. I bought Salim Ali's famous book of birds. The garden was refreshing and charming, with roses, dahlias, hibiscus and bougainvillea. Sometimes the gardener catnapped at noon in the shade of our lime tree.

Wandering salesmen approached the gate and beamed their hopeful smiles. Parakeet cages festooned the bird-seller's bicycle. A basket maker set out his bike-load of cane tables in the drive. He nimbly jumped up and down on them, striking balletic poses to emphasize their strength. A man came with a monkey which played a drum. A brace of drifting priests offered inexpensive prayers. Astrologers called from time to time to dispense hope and guidance and a look into the future. All events in India, great and small, involve advice from the stargazers: marriage, pregnancy, a foreign trip, starting a business, making a film, building a bridge, ploughing a field. The pearl that politicians wear is bought on an astrologer's advice. No one would arrange anything important at the time of an eclipse. When the stars and moon are in agreement, the wedding season begins.

A white-bearded Sikh tailor eased himself from the creaking pillion of a motorbike. His shirt pockets bulged with pens, spectacles and tape measures. He was a sort of regimental tailor to the foreign correspondents. His speciality was a short sleeve bush shirt with four capacious pockets, ideal for travelling light. As he measured my waist, he murmured that men should not be thin. His own belly was majestic. He said it grew from butter-love, and that mine would expand for the same reason. I insisted that trousers should fit my waist.

'I am telling you,' he sighed, 'that when you are eating more butter you will be telephoning me and saying: 'Mr Singh, my pant is too tight.'

Our veranda faced a maidan, a village green bordered on three sides by houses, gardens and handsome shady trees. At the far end of it, taxi drivers slept, night and day, on the back seats of their cars, so that a taxi sometimes had the scent of a warm and pungent sock. In winter, the drivers tied their headscarves snugly around their chins in the Sandringham manner.

The maidan was good for cricket. As I read and wrote on the veranda, I heard the crack of the ball. A white ox hauled a mower. Women sat in circles on the grass, their laughter tinkling like a tambourine. A languor of musicians snoozed among their sousaphones and drums. Soon a bridegroom arrived on a white horse, a prince for a day, and the bandsmen roused themselves to play him to his wedding. Strolling families, meanwhile, sculpted ice cream cornets with their tongues. Skinny ice-wallahs pedalled slowly by, their buttocks cooled by dripping blocks of ice roped beneath their saddles. Mangoes, too, soothed monsoon suffering. Connoisseurs favoured Alfonsos and Bombay Green, Langra and Fruit of Paradise, Parrot-fairy and Collector Sahib. Nehru used to send a treat of Dussehris to the Queen.

My office ceiling fan slowly churned the air. I finished writing early in the evening and drove through the part of Delhi called New Delhi that Lutyens and Baker built in the 1920s and 1930s. Soon I was swept into the tide of capsizing buses, belching trucks and three-wheeled cabs stuffed with humanity. Each weaving motor scooter was an epic of family life: father drove, his son stood between his knees, his wife sat side-saddle in a sari, a baby on her knee, a daughter clinging to her waist. Through the chaos swayed imperturbable elephants. During my first year in Delhi the sky was still blue. In later years, it developed a cloak of exhaust fumes. I discussed this with a businessman. 'It is you Westerners who worry about pollution,' he said, 'our lungs are used to it.' Still, Delhi had a notable guttural cough, the tree leaves became coated with grime and elephant keepers no longer took their animals to the river to bathe. The water was too dirty.

I took my typed copy to the Associated Press office in the city centre. These were the years BC: before computers. An operator tapped out a telex tape of my story and fed it into the teleprinter. After a pause, the machine chattered out the answer code 264971 Times G. The story was on its way, a good feeling. The time in Delhi was five-and-a-half hours ahead of London. I liked that time of day, the warmth of the evening, the gossip of the American correspondents, the clatter of typewriter and telex, something satisfyingly inky and journalistic.

On the whole, London left me to my own devices and allowed me to paint my own portrait of India and to travel, within reason, where I wished. I naturally wrote about the unfolding political events, the backbone of coverage of any country, but there was also a strong appetite for stories communicating the colour and flavour of India: readable tales about people which needed no particular news peg and sometimes involved journeys to distant places. I felt in the early weeks that it had all the promise of adventure and a privileged education, learning on the hoof. I was not disappointed.

Many readers of *The Times* knew something of India. They had, perhaps, soldiered, worked and travelled there, had eaten the curry. They liked to follow the unfolding story. I met many who, in retirement, enjoyed a journey to the country they had known when young. India was also a land of interest for young people who trekked and travelled its vastness. I, too, embraced the adventure of it all, the story, exhilarated by my freedom to journey, discover and report. When I started reporting the subcontinent, modern India and Pakistan were thirty-two years old. People in their forties and fifties held vivid memories of the massacres that followed Britain's partitioning of the subcontinent into two independent countries. Millions of Hindus fled across the new frontier to India, millions of Muslims surged from India into Pakistan. More than half a million died in the slaughter. People remembered the trains leaking blood when they arrived at stations.

In my office at home, I stared every day at the great chart on my wall and wondered: where next? I travelled everywhere with my indispensable portable typewriter. We shared adventures. On it I wrote of everything I saw. Planes left Delhi early and I was often in the air by six, on the way to a new place. I learned the patience of the long-distance telex man, waiting for 264971 to appear, amid the power cuts, feeling like a gambler at the roulette wheel. Once, when I landed at Delhi an airport official took my typewriter away. 'Sir, it is confiscated for your own good,' he said in explanation. He returned it eventually. Its case is cracked and taped and covered with the stickers of forgotten airlines. I still use it from time to time, for its magic properties, of course: I have come to believe that it is itself a casket of words.

A telex message said my father was seriously ill. At the airport, I found I had arrived with my second passport. This lacked the stamp recording my arrival in India. Naturally the official noticed the discrepancy. 'Since you have not arrived,' he said, reasonably, 'how can you leave?' I showed him the telex message, the news of my father's illness. He applied the exit stamp. 'At such a time,' he said, 'a son's place is with his father.' A few days after the funeral I returned to Delhi.

★

Our home was the lower floor of a tree-shaded house. The Singh family, Brijendra, Dawn and their daughter, Ambika, had the upper floors. Brijendra was our landlord. He worked as a conservationist and was an honorary ranger in the forests of Corbett Park, about 150 miles from Delhi. The park took its name from the adventurer and author Jim Corbett who hunted tigers and leopards there for thirty-two years from 1907. Dawn was the daughter of Dutch missionaries. She and her sister were orphaned when they were little girls and were then raised in the family of an Indian cabinet secretary.

Brijendra belonged to the princely family of Kapurthala in Punjab. The colonial British ruled India with the co-operation of 565 maharajas, rajas, ranas, rawats, raos, maharaos, jams, mirs, khans, nizams and nawabs whose lands covered three-fifths of the country. Many of these rulers were wealthy. The British forbade them to style themselves royal. They could not be addressed as majesty, or wear a crown or call a chair a throne. Some princes improved the lives of their subjects. Most did little. At independence in 1947, the princes extinguished themselves as rulers. Some went into politics and business and palace tourism.

Brijendra devoted himself to Corbett wildlife, particularly the conservation of tigers. These magnificent creatures were ruthlessly and illegally hunted for their skins, bones and organs, believed in China and elsewhere to be remedies for a flagging libido.

India banned hunting, but the enemies of tigers multiplied. Black market dealers encouraged poaching. Demand for land and water squeezed the tigers' habitat. Male tigers could not roam to find mates. Brijendra made the point that tigers are good for you, that to save the tiger you have to save its habitat of life-sustaining forests and rivers.

He invited us to join him at Corbett. As we drove through the forest in the dark, a sinewy tiger, 'burning bright', bounded across our track. Early next morning we were sitting on howdahs on the backs of two elephants, moving through tall grass towards the jungle in a swaying rhythm. Mahouts and forest rangers stared intently at the ground, looking for blood. After an hour, the elephants abruptly stopped. Mahouts pointed to broken bamboo and splashes of blood. A tiger had felled a deer and dragged it away. The mahouts urged the elephants forward, following the drag trail to a stream. On the other side was a skull gnawed clean.

Now the elephants were still. We hardly dared to breathe. From the grass came a long, low growl. Hair prickled on the back of my neck. We could not see the tigress. But through the grass we spied her cub's black and amber face. Ten feet up on the howdah we were fairly safe. The mahouts steered the elephants away.

A day later we followed another trail of blood spots. We stopped suddenly. The mahout pointed. As I stared into the pattern of sunlight and shadow I saw a tiger's satin skin. I realized I was looking into her eyes. After a minute or two she walked from cover, faced us as if in disdainful inspection, then strolled away, supple and shining. It was thrilling. The first tiger is unforgettable.

Some time later I met a Corbett mahout, Subedar Ali, at Brijendra's home in Delhi. His head was heavily bandaged. With Dawn as his interpreter, he told me his story.

In the forest, he said, he dismounted from his elephant to cut fodder. He had just started when a tiger seized him. He saw his torn–off scalp in its jaws. The tiger straddled him, slashed at his back and ripped off his left ear. He had only seconds to live. He punched the tiger's head. At that moment, another mahout on an elephant charged and drove the tiger off. Subedar Ali was scooped up by his own elephant. Brijendra brought him to Delhi to be repaired by surgeons.

★

I was introduced to a distinguished Sikh who lived nearby. His name was Hardit Singh Malik and he was eighty-eight when he related to me the remarkable story of his life. He remembered Edwardian London, horse buses and hansom cabs. At thirteen, he was a real-life model of the exotic boys from India portrayed in British school stories. He was educated at Eastbourne college. 'I was well up with Latin and Greek because I had a tutor at home in India. I went to Balliol in 1912 and graduated with honours in history. In August 1914, I played cricket for Sussex against Kent and scored twenty-five. The other reason I remember the match is that war was declared on the second day. I joined the French Red Cross and became an ambulance driver.'

As a trainee pilot in the Royal Flying Corps in 1917, he wore an outsize flying helmet over his turban. Known as 'the flying Sikh', he was one of four Indians in the RFC and went to France after twenty hours' tuition.

'I really learnt to fly in battle. Many of us were shot down. I was lucky to be under the command of Captain William Barker VC. He looked after novices like me. I shot down one of the Baron von Richthofen squadron, then crash-landed behind our lines with 400 bullet holes in my plane.' No one, he said with a smile, ever got his turban, not the ragging schoolboys at Eastbourne, the sergeant at Aldershot or the German fighter pilots. In England, in 1921, he played cricket for Sussex and scored a century against Leicestershire. He left England to make his career in the Indian Civil Service. From 1949 to 1956, he was India's ambassador to France.

★

In the hot weather, I always found good reasons to travel to the hills: to Dharmsala to interview the Dalai Lama, to Chail to play cricket on the highest cricket ground in India, to the Western Ghats, to Gilgit, to the plantation country in Sri Lanka and the hill country above Chittagong, to Kashmir, the Karakoram Highway, to Pokhara in Nepal where Gurkhas were recruited. Up the serpentine road in the Nilgiri Hills, past the sign that read: Sleeping While Driving Is Strictly Prohibited, my wife and I made a pilgrimage of a kind to the Ooty Club, the birthplace of snooker. As I signed the register, a servant showed me a card reminding me of Rule 13, that I could not dine at the club unless I was suitably dressed. I persuaded the manager of a nearby hotel to lend me a jacket. It was small and tight, and the tie that came with it was garish, but both passed muster. I bent reverently to my cue on the faded baize. Like so many relics of the Raj, the club echoed to footfalls and was itself an echo, the old stronghold of a vanished caste. In an empty dining room, beneath the mounted heads of tigers and snarling jackals, we had celery soup, baked fish, roasted chicken and lemon tart, served by an immaculate and silent man. I smiled when I read the old complaints book, imagining those crusty sahibs in their throttling collars harrumphing over their pegs of whisky as they wrote: 'Only three courses for lunch today!' 'The peas contained live worms, this completely upset the appetite at the table.' 'No cheese again for lunch!' And 'The table was cleared of drinks while we were dancing.' The membership was dwindling, but the club, when we stayed there, remained courtly, formal and hospitable.

★

Kuldip Nayar and Khushwant Singh were the Indian journalists I knew best. They were both Punjabis who fled from Pakistan to India during the massacres of partition in 1947. Starting out as lawyers, they both became journalists, editors and authors, and were pioneering syndicated columnists.

Kuldip was twenty-three, a doctor's son, when he left home amid the murderous chaos of partition. 'We thought we would be able to travel between Pakistan and India as easily as you do between England and Wales. In our house I left my copy of *War and Peace*, and my mother her best shawl, thinking we would return. We never did and lost everything. I saw rivers of humanity streaming into Pakistan and India, hundreds of thousands, terrified.'

Khushwant also had a perilously close view of partition violence in Punjab. He left a train just before murderers attacked it and killed every Sikh aboard. He reached Delhi in August in time to see independence declared. He set his best-selling novel, *Train to Pakistan*, in the violence of partition. It was not surprising that half a century passed before the novel was filmed.

'So much blood and sorrow,' Khushwant brooded when I talked to him on the fiftieth anniversary of 1947. 'Fifty monsoons cannot wash them away.'

He was a leading journalist for nearly forty years and sought always to be frank. He revolutionized Indian magazine journalism. His sexual candour sometimes dismayed his admirers. He was a veteran foe of religious intolerance. As a Sikh who wrote critically of Sikh extremists, he earned death threats and an armed guard. He was an Indian who accepted the unpopularity of speaking up for Pakistan. Someone in Canada once addressed a letter: Khushwant Singh, Bastard, India. It reached his home in Delhi.

Always a believer in India's secular ideal, he denounced extremists during the Sikh insurgency in the 1980s: 'I could talk to my community because I was part of it.' He protested strongly against Mrs Gandhi's ordering of the bloody army assault on the Sikhs' holiest place, the Golden Temple. When her Sikh bodyguards killed her in her garden in 1984, Hindu mobs murdered hundreds of Sikhs in Delhi. Khushwant was a marked man because he was a Sikh. Just in time, the Swedish

A photo lesson in Rajasthan

My mother and father on their engagement day

Man and microphone: my father in his singing heyday

The author, aged eight

Calcutta station: a boy curls up to sleep beside a steam locomotive

Interview with the exiled Dalai Lama, leader of Tibetan Buddhists, at his home in the Himalaya foothills

Perched like a bird on a step an old man watches street life in Jaisalmer, Rajasthan

At Cape Comorin in south India, a pilgrim bears his burden

A woman wears her wealth in Jaipur

The art of the turban, silk or cotton, many different styles … this one red

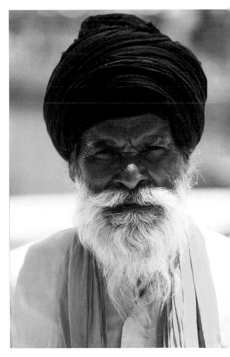

… and this one blue

In the water paradise of Kashmir women paddle their way to market

embassy in Delhi gave him sanctuary. For more than ten years, police guarded his home; when I called on him, I showed the stern sentries the Scotch I had brought, and they gave the slightest of smiles. Khushwant died in Delhi aged ninety-nine, writing to the end.

★

Journalism, Mark Tully told me, had not given him a proper life, but India certainly had. The son of a businessman, he was born in Calcutta in 1935 and educated at a boarding school in Darjeeling. He was ten when he went to England. He studied for the church, but his teachers decided he was not the right sort. 'I was a bit wild. It was partly a matter of liking beer too much, partly of doubts.'

In 1964 the BBC sent him to Delhi as an administrator but he soon turned himself into a broadcaster and embraced the job of the BBC's India staff correspondent for thirty years. He knew from the first day that in India he had found his home, the place where he felt he belonged. His reports had authority and clarity. He had great gusto and a famous voice. People called him 'Tully sahib.'

When Mrs Gandhi, in her authoritarian spell in 1975, banished him from India, Mark Tully felt he had been turned out of his home. He spent a miserable eighteen months waiting to go back. When I started reporting India and got to know him, he was ever hospitable and candid, one of those who helped me to understand a vast and complex society and country.

Although, at first, he thought British rule was excellent, he changed his mind. He defended the caste system that evolved over 3,000 years as part of India's fibre, providing community, identity, kinship and self-respect. He rejected the idea that Britain did a lot for India. To his mind, the Raj acted in its own interests and applied inappropriate Western remedies to India's problems. 'The Raj,' he thought, 'could not have survived if the British had not created an Indian elite convinced that British culture was inherently superior to that of India. I look forward to an Indian renaissance, making its own way in life.'

He said he was glad he was 'emotionally more of a Mahatma Gandhi man than a Nehru one. It is inconceivable that I should break my link with India. One of the reasons I like it here is that there is something to hope for'.

★

Of course, I wrote often about Mrs Gandhi. She disliked talking to reporters. A Western journalist interviewed her and asked her if, like many Indian people, she meditated. 'Yes,' she said, 'I find I am meditating during this interview.'

On the eve of an official visit to Britain, she agreed to talk to me, but said little about the politics of it all. She became animated, though, when we talked of London, which she knew and liked in her youth: 'My people are trying to schedule a theatre visit, to see *Cats*. Have you seen it? Is it good? And will there still be daffodils in the park?'

★

When Mahatma Gandhi was seven, his father was appointed finance minister to the ruler of Rajkot in Gujarat. The boy went to the Alfred High School in the city from 1880-87. A marble plaque proclaims its distinguished old boy as Mahatma in the Making. In the school's gloomy main hall, a dog-eared display of reports showed that Gandhi was an indifferent pupil. I wished to visit the city museum nearby, but it was closed for a holiday. 'You must be knowing,' said the exasperated man who had promised to show it to me, 'that everyone wants a job in government because it is a life of holidays and idle chat and going for tea and not caring about the wants of the people.'

One evening I had a hotel to myself, eating dinner in solitary splendour at a long table with room for twenty or more. A waiter on my left served the meal, another on my right cleared the dishes, the manager sat in front of me, not eating but watching. As I lay in my grand brass bedstead next morning, I heard film music and high-pitched singing. It was just before five o'clock. Tambourines and bells suddenly struck up, playing an accompaniment to a repetitive chant in praise of a god. This roused the lion in the travelling circus across the road. He gave vent, not to a roar, but to a deep groaning in his gut. This caused the silly peacocks in the palace grounds to utter sharp 'Miaow,

miaow' calls, like children imitating cats. Soon a muezzin switched on the loudspeakers in the nearby mosque, cleared his throat fruitily and launched a penetrating call to prayer. To the unorchestrated jingle of the tambourine, the chanting, the film song, the lion's intestinal tuba, the peacocks' mewing and the muezzin's cry, there was added the earwax-cracking whistle of a train. There is no sense in taking an alarm clock to India.

★

In Calcutta, I talked to Mother Teresa about her thirty years of work among the city's destitute and dying, and her home for foundlings and unmarried mothers. I thanked her for giving me time to discuss it all and she smiled gently. 'Even a journalist,' she said, 'can do the work of the Lord.'

★

In Cochin, the warm southern air had the distinctive scent of coconut, fish and spices. I ducked into a courtroom and soon felt a rill of perspiration between my shoulders. The prisoner sat in a dock that looked like an oversize playpen. The magistrate, writing patiently, wore a wing collar, a black jacket and gown and an air of dignity. A white shirt covered the prosecutor's aldermanic paunch. He, too, wore a wing collar and bands at his neck, a black jacket and a torn gown. His flared trousers were a startling blue and on his feet were rubber flip-flops. He wiggled his toes and stroked his moustache. He spoke, of course, mellifluous Malayalam which bubbled like a stream. He cross-examined the witness who wore a turquoise shirt and a long cotton lungi. A woman sitting near the witness stand discreetly breastfed the baby lying in the folds of her pink sari. A couple of policemen in voluminous shorts put their heads together and grinned. Anyone who has sat in a court in Britain would have recognized the scene. Here British jurisprudence was blended with Indian colour and custom and spice. Outside, barebacked men walked the waterfront bearing baskets of fish on their heads. A large, rusting ship sounded its siren as it passed the fishing boats. Masses of water hyacinths swirled in the tidal stream.

I drove down the coast to Alleppey to board a converted rice boat. It was sixty years old and built of teak. The sleeping cabin and saloon had a roof of bamboo and wattle fashioned in a distinctive hump. A group of rice boats looked like a convocation of turtles. A crew of four looked after me, the captain, the cook, the engineer and the guide. The craft was powered by bamboo poles and a small outboard. The boat's library consisted of a paperback copy of Dickens's *Hard Times*, so I had Mr Gradgrind for company.

Much of the spirit of Kerala lies in its waterlands: lakes, canals and shallow fens sluiced by more than forty rivers running down from the hills. For three months each year, the monsoon rains drench everything and the land bursts with a brilliant fecundity.

Late in the afternoon we stopped at a creek-side toddy shop, a hut with wooden benches on an earth floor. Four men, shoulders shaking with excitement, played a game with mussel shells on a board scratched in the earth. The pot-bellied barman hoisted a plastic can of toddy, the fermented sap of the coconut palm, and dribbled it through a strainer into glasses. It tasted rank and undrinkable. My guide tossed it back with relish. In the hour before dusk the boat was anchored in a broad lagoon. The crew lit oil lamps and cooked a fish curry with coconut and rice and banana fritters. I stretched out on the foredeck mattress and, by lamplight, read a few pages of Mr Gradgrind. Lamps flickered on Chinese fishing nets, a legacy of Kerala's ancient trade with China, like the cooking woks and the conical hats of boatmen. I rose at five o'clock to watch the sunrise. The crew jumped over the side for their bath, then brought tea and a peppery omelette.

This was not my first visit to Cochin. I had been here briefly with my wife some months before. I remembered that an effusive hotel manager had installed us in the honeymoon suite, a large high-ceilinged room. To our right, as we stood on the threshold, was a dark brown cocktail bar without a single bottle. In the distance, to our left, were two narrow beds, hard enough to suit penitential monks. Between the bar and the beds in this honeymoon suite was a ping-pong table.

Chapter 7

A walk to Tora Bora

In Pakistan I wrote from Lahore, Islamabad, Rawalpindi, Karachi and Quetta. Most frequently I reported from Peshawar. It never disappointed. Its valley formed the great oasis of the north-west frontier. It had been a trading place in the second century and was the chief city of the Pathan people in the eighth century. The Khyber Pass winds sinuously through a dramatic brown landscape, a broken terrain bristling with forts.

The men are striking. They wear beards and bandoliers, smocks and pantaloons, turbans, filigree caps and piecrust berets called pakols. They have large, sandalled feet, accipitrine faces, dark eyes; but, sometimes, irises of green or blue. A rigid rule of honour governs Pathan tribal life. There is the code of revenge, called badal, and the code of hospitality called pakhtunwali.

No bazaar in Asia is more picturesque than Peshawar, a maze of smoky streets, metal workshops, tailors, tea houses and chicken dinners. I learned of it first when I was a schoolboy and read a novel called *The Slave of the Khan*, set in Peshawar and the Khyber. The book is quite tattered now, but readable.

The British built their orderly cantonment as relief from the seething city. I took a tonga, a two-wheeled pony taxi, to ride along the Mall. A military order prevailed: traffic cops and white lines, shady trees in disciplined ranks. A sign commanded: No Horns Please, Silence is Gold. Another said simply: Smile.

To see the Khyber Pass I rented a car with a driver and bought a £2 permit which included the obligatory services of a Khyber levy, a youth of the Afridi tribe. He was my bodyguard. Armed with a rifle, he sat in the front with the driver. We set out in fierce heat and entered the lion-coloured Khyber, a harsh stretch of shimmering rock and scrub. The people live behind steel gates in mud-walled compounds with watchtowers. Columns of women walked across fields carrying loads of fodder.

The road twisted through cliffs and rocks decorated with the regimental crests of British soldiers who marched here in the nineteenth century. Carved in the rock were the badges of the South Wales Borderers, the Gordon Highlanders, the Essex Regiment and others. I imagined the troops in their khaki sweating and swearing. The driver took me to the fort at Michni, 3,600 feet up, and I looked towards the Plain of Jalalabad and the lunar landscape of the Hindu Kush.

Later I hired a Jeep and driver and set off for the Malakand Pass, following in Churchill's footsteps. He was here in 1897, a subaltern aged twenty-three, fighting against tribesmen. Moonlighting as a correspondent for *The Daily Telegraph*, he wrote for £5 a column. 'The British officer,' he wrote in one report, 'was spinning around, his face a mass of blood, his right eye cut out. Yes, it certainly was an adventure.'

The road to Malakand passed through a tapestry of orchards, rice paddies and sugar cane fields. My driver added his toots to the fanfaronades of trucks and wheezing buses. Heading into the Swat Valley, I saw on a bluff a white fortress known as Churchill's Picquet. I entered it and looked through a gunport at the river below. A plaque informed me that the room was 'Churchill's abode ... from where he used to send dispatches to London as a war correspondent in 1897'.

At Charsadda, on the road to Malakand, I visited Khan Abdul Ghaffar Khan, almost ninety then, the greatest living witness of the old frontier. Tall and impressive, a Pathan leader, he was a follower of Mahatma Gandhi and known as the Frontier Gandhi. The British jailed him for his part in the struggle for independence. When I called on him he was dignified and courteous and would not talk until I had been served tea and biscuits. 'I have been a fighter all my life,' he said sadly. 'I wanted to knit the divided tribes into one brotherhood and wish I could have done more. So, if you want to know how I feel, in the last part of my life, ask yourself how you would feel.'

I went south to the Kohat Pass, another spectacular road of precipitous cliffs, and found the white-domed residence of Sir Louis Cavagnari, who was in charge of the district in 1866-7. He was later the British envoy in Kabul and was killed there in 1879, his death triggering the Afghan war of that year, a British disaster.

★

In 1982 I flew from Rawalpindi to Gilgit in a Fokker Friendship, a thrilling flight through the mountains, with a long circuit around the great peak of Nanga Parbat. I went to talk to the Kirghiz, a nomadic tribe of 1,100 people, packing their bags and cooking pots to begin a remarkable migration. As refugees in Gilgit, they were too warm. Warmth and malaria were killing them. As picturesque herding people, they could live only in cold weather on high mountains. They were leaving Gilgit for a new life in the wintry slopes of eastern Turkey. They would board a bus to Rawalpindi and from there would fly to Turkey. Their leader told me: 'I think I'm about 70, still strong enough to lead my people to a new life.'

Bad weather closed Gilgit to aircraft, and I and three other travellers opted to return to Rawalpindi by car. Knowing that the journey would last twelve hours, I asked the car agent if there were an assistant driver. 'Oh, yes,' he said. 'Can he drive?' I asked. 'No,' he said. 'If he sees the driver is sleeping he hits him on the shoulder.' We had little choice and set off on the Karakoram Highway, the highest road in the world, where the Hindu Kush, the Pamirs, Himalayas and Karakorams meet. This is ancient Silk Road country. Thousands of Pakistani and Chinese men had just completed the highway project and had opened the Khunjerab Pass which links China and Pakistan. Karakoram means crumbling rock. Our car picked its way around fallen boulders and was once dug out of the sand. We stopped at checkpoints to show our passports and state our profession. One of my companions declared straight-faced that he was a lion tamer. I was greatly relieved to get back to Rawalpindi.

★

After the Soviet invasion of Afghanistan in December 1979 more than two million Afghans, men, women and children, fled to the Peshawar

Valley and elsewhere in Pakistan. Refugee camps grew into crowded towns. The mujahidin, the fighting men, came here from the battlefields to see their families. Fighters maimed in action limped along narrow mountain paths, staggering on crutches to reach hospitals in Peshawar. I remember two boys of fifteen, both shot through the abdomen, brought over the frontier on camels. Other wounded boys and men told me their stories, showed me their bandaged bullet wounds and the stumps left by landmine blasts that blew off their feet and hands. In Peshawar one day, returning fighters showed me a basket filled with small Russian mines, the explosive traps laid on mountain paths that could cripple a man. They produced the paybooks of young Russian soldiers killed or taken prisoner in the fighting.

Foreign correspondents reporting the war in Afghanistan knew that much of the information emerging was a wash of rumour and unreliable reports. In the dusty Peshawar offices of the Afghan fighters a spokesman would say: 'We bring you news from the fighting front.' It was difficult or impossible to verify any of it. Like most correspondents, I travelled to Peshawar because it was close to the action, the Afghan frontier only thirty miles from the city.

In the spring of 1981, fighting had been raging for fifteen months. I and my friend Tyler Marshall, a correspondent for the *Los Angeles Times*, believed that a journey on foot over the mountains into Afghanistan, seeing the fighting, landscape and people at first hand, would be invaluable, better than anything the Peshawar briefings had to offer.

We met Pathan elders in a gloomy room in Peshawar, told them we wished to see the war through the eyes of the mujahidin, and asked for their help in crossing the mountains. They listened in silence and left the room. We waited through the afternoon. Towards sunset, a man entered. 'Yes,' he said softly, 'we can help you to reach the fighting front.'

Next day we bought grey and grubby long-tailed shirts and baggy trousers from mujahidin fighters. In the city bazaar we bought thin brown blankets and berets. Into shabby canvas haversacks we put cameras, large rolls of plaster to repair our feet, and the minimum of spare clothing.

'Wait at Dean's hotel,' we were instructed, 'there will be a signal.' We ate Dean's popular dinner of mulligatawny soup and chicken, and had it again the next day. Three days later a ratatat on the door made us jump. A pair of Afghan Pathans hovered on the veranda beside the flowerbeds.

'Come, mister.'

Following them through Peshawar's puzzle of streets, we came to a battered bus painted with scenes of snowy mountains and a sign saying: The owner of this bus is God. Our minders shochorned us in. The greybeards already crammed on the benches glared like affronted eagles. We submerged beneath our blankets and feigned sleep, invisible among the dozing Afghans and the heap of luggage.

The bus yawed through the twisting Khyber for a couple of hours, its horn bugling all the way. It stopped at Landi Kotal, a bustling business and smuggling town. Our guides led us to open ground among rocks where young men were clambering eagerly into lorries. The light was fading. Hands reached down to pull us aboard a cattle truck filled with more than thirty jostling Afghans. They carried bundles of clothing and new square-toed sandals for men on the battlefield. Their leader shook hands with us. He wore a pinstripe jacket and carried a Kalashnikov, the only man in our group with a firearm.

The truck toiled uphill and stopped. Our companions said their prayers and started walking. Afraid of faltering in the darkness, we fixed our gaze on the heels ahead. This was a relentless march with men we did not know who spoke words we did not understand. Later, in the blackness, a voice murmured, 'Afghanistan.' We were over the border. No one stopped. We faced inward on a narrow ledge and inched for fifty yards across a cliff. Thin torch beams pricked the night. Just after transiting the cliff, I slipped suddenly on scree. Two men grasped my arms at once, took my pack and kept me walking.

Some hours later, we reached a dry creek and rested. The mujahidin nibbled food from their pockets, fragments of bread and hard brown sugar. One of them leaned over a stagnant puddle on a smooth rock. He broke the scum with his forefinger, then knelt and dipped his tongue like a cat.

Around two in the morning we started walking again, absorbing the pain in our knees.

Dawn disclosed majestic beauty, a valley, a river sparkling in a curving canyon, distant snowy peaks. Before us were lush pocket-sized fields, irrigated balconies and ledges for fruit, rice and corn. Goats and fat-tailed sheep grazed. Chickens scratched.

As we entered a village, around seven o'clock, smiling men emerged from mud-brick houses bearing cups of sugary tea. They showed us the shredded remnants of rockets fired by a helicopter. We drank more tea poured from blue and yellow pots. As guests, we received extra sugar.

'Sterreh musheh,' the village men called as we set off. The words mean 'May you never tire.' We met mujahidin on the march, their chests crossed by bandoliers. They raised their Kalashnikovs, posing for our cameras.

'Sterreh musheh,' they called.

'Sterreh musheh,' we answered.

'Walk, mister,' our Pathans prodded, 'walk.'

We heard a rolling thunder of distant artillery. That evening we came to a village. The people gave us bread dipped in curd. We slept on charpoys. At dawn, we drank tea and sucked sweets. In a couple of hours, we stood concealed by a wall and looked across a valley as a wheeling helicopter fired rockets into a village.

More than anything, the mujahidin feared ambush from the air. We crossed dry rivers in threes and fours, 100 yards apart. On mountain tracks, we avoided grouping. As we climbed a high path that morning, our companions tugged our sleeves and pushed us into scrub and boulders. 'Helicopter.' Covered in our brown blankets, we huddled as still as rocks. The rotors chopped overhead. That afternoon, a fear that enemy troops were active forced us to wait. Guides led us in silence through darkness to a remote and ruined mosque. Thirty of us slept in a chaos of arms and legs. We marched at six, and at eleven stopped in a village and ate an omelette.

Seventy-two hours after leaving the Khyber, we walked in single file up the long and narrow trail to Tora Bora, a mountain stronghold south of Jalalabad. The doctor, aged twenty-four, was dabbing iodine on cuts and gashes caused by a recent rocket attack. We slept under pungent quilts and awoke to drink green tea. We had bread made on a sheet of iron, and beans and rice moistened by bitter orange juice. The mujahidin here, around 200 of them, lived in small caves, mudbrick shelters and dugouts. They had captured Soviet machine guns and rocket launchers, and had recently hauled a twin-barrelled cannon up the mountain path. They prayed five times a day.

Their commander, Abdul Khayam, a former geography teacher in his thirties, spoke English. 'Tora Bora is our Kabul,' he said, 'our capital. From here we fight forever. You are British, you know how we defeated the British army, and you know why we will win this war against the Russians. You British could tell them. They have not learned the lesson of history. We fight on our own land and grow stronger.'

He and his men waged war by ambush, stealing Russian weapons and ammunition. Their numbers grew as men in the Afghan army gathered weapons and deserted to join the mujahidin. From the West, they wanted launchers and missiles to fight the helicopters. Eventually they received them.

We spent three days in Tora Bora. A man called Arif said he would lead us down to the plain and find a guide to take us to Pakistan. Arif was impressively barrel-chested, built for the front of the scrum. He looked rather like Stanley Baker. His black beard gleamed and blue eyes glittered. With his Kalashnikov, bandoliers and two spare magazines in his belt he was the picture of a tribal guerrilla.

Arif said that he wanted to get on with fighting the Russians. He genially hoped to see the back of us as soon as possible. In the meantime, we descended the track to a fast-flowing stream and picked our way through rocket-riddled hamlets. We stopped in a field to watch three farmers meticulously harvesting opium from poppies, cutting the pods with razors to extract a milky ooze.

Raw opium, purified and refined, was channelled through Pakistan to fund the mujahidin war against the Russians. In time this trade made Pakistan the leading world source of heroin, making rich men of Afghan warlords and providing farmers and their families with an income.

Arif ushered us into a house near Jalalabad for a meal. We had eaten barely a mouthful when a youth whispered to him. He sprang up, grasped his rifle and ordered us to follow. We could barely keep up, running and tripping, desperate in the dark. We ran maybe two miles and stumbled into a fortified house. Our chests ached. We were exhausted.

'Here,' Arif panted, 'safe.'

Our new hosts gave us tea, bread to dip into curd and spinach and charpoys to rest on. In our run through the darkness, I had dropped my blanket. Our hosts sent a boy out to retrieve it. In half an hour, he brought it back. On the edge of sleep, I was aware of Arif and our hosts talking quietly, and the hiss of their spittle in the fire. Stirring before daybreak, I saw Arif rise. He shouldered his gun and left in silence. He was absent for seven hours. To our relief, he returned in the company of a small man and a gangling youth. Arif said the small man was Saddaq and he would be our guide. Saddaq was as jaunty as a squirrel. He looked at us and smiled. He wore a long, sky-blue shirt and a turban loosely tied. He walked nimbly in black Ali Baba shoes with a curly point at the toe. He knew not a word of English. Arif explained that Saddaq was a smuggler, running Afghan opium to his clients in the Khyber.

We reasoned that Saddaq's survival depended on his reliability. His clients had to trust him, we had to trust him, too. There was no choice. I was relieved to see that Saddaq was unarmed. It was safer that way.

Arif was pleased that he had honoured his obligation. We now had a guide and were ready to go. Saddaq tied a large cake of opium as big as a French cheese onto the back of his human mule. He called for a chillum, a water pipe, and squatted to smoke it. The hashish detonated an explosion of coughing. He sprang up, gasping, eyes streaming, legs moving like pistons. He and his galloping mule hurried away. We struggled to keep up. Arif laughed. 'Walk, mister,' he cried. 'Walk.' He raised his rifle in farewell.

That evening, and the two following evenings, Saddaq found us shelter: a house, an earth floor, a quilt, tea, bread and a rare egg. To our hosts he was well-known. The following day we reached a broad river. Saddaq and his boy hoisted us onto their backs and carried us over as quickly as possible.

Saddaq started each day with a blast from the chillum, the tears rolling down his cheeks. He climbed rhythmically up the paths and rocks. We took some hours to reach the top of the last mountain. At the summit, he pointed ahead. 'Pakistan zindabad,' he said, 'Pakistan forever.' Some hours later, we found a bus waiting on a rough road, bound for Landi Kotal with travellers from Afghanistan. The driver, however, refused to start the engine. The passengers sat with folded arms, complaining that the fare was too high and they would not pay. We bridged the impasse by paying the difference for everyone. Nobody lost face. The driver started the engine.

At Landi Kotal, we said farewell to Saddaq. As agreed, we paid him £15 each for guiding us. He smiled and waved. We owed a debt to Arif and to Saddaq and to pakhtunwali. We boarded a bus for Peshawar. We had been out of contact for two weeks. At Dean's, I retrieved my typewriter and sent a telex to *The Times*: 'Rebased Peshawar.'

I kept a small notebook in Afghanistan. I read it for a while and began to type.

'The blackened rubble of Tora Bora war camp bears witness to its importance as a mujahidin base. Russian gunships have bombed and rocketed it many times; the doctor is still swabbing stinging iodine on shrapnel gashes after the last raid, but the guerrillas are grinning and their black and white flag flies jauntily, a sort of thumbed nose. The Russians have failed to blast them from their mountain crevices and mujahidin confidence and capability are growing.'

We had seen for ourselves a fragment of the struggle and the people involved in it. We could not know that it would last nine years. The poppies, meanwhile, grew in profusion and would generate great wealth for the extreme Taliban movement which emerged among Afghan Pathans at the end of 1994.

Chapter 8

The bandit king

Two hundred miles south of Delhi, where the Chambal river flows, I went looking for bandits. It was not too difficult. I found one quite soon, in a small town. He smiled an icy smile and said he was Madho Singh. A retired bandit, he emphasized. Having murdered ten men, he quit the criminal life, surrendered to the police and served a jail sentence. Now he was a ransom-broker mediating between heartless kidnappers and the desperate parents of stolen sons. As a sideline, he was working as a conjuror.

Over countless centuries, the Chambal and its sister streams chiselled the soft brown rock into labyrinthine canyons up to 250 feet deep. In these ravines the shadowy jungle conceals wild pigs and lawless men. Dacoit is the Hindi word for robber, but Chambal bandits have often had a lofty idea of their status and strutted under the name of baghis. Since this means rebels, they seemed to market themselves as versions of Robin Hood or Jesse James or Ned Kelly.

I first saw the river's hinterland in 1980, when the police of central India were under political pressure to round up more of the kidnappers and killers. A much-decorated veteran officer said to me that the only practical way to deal with bandits was to shoot them. Bandit gangs, however, had their uses as private armies in territory where caste conflict was embedded. They also had money. Their ability and willingness to pay high prices for meat, whisky and ammunition benefited friendly villages. As well as buying food, such bandits gave money to local temples and arbitrated in disputes. In the villages of Madhya Pradesh and Rajasthan, dacoits moved easily enough among their own castes, exploiting the people's loyalty and fear. They had glamour and power.

'You learn the telltale signs when dacoits arrive in a village,' a police officer said to me. 'You sense the buzz of excitement. The people may tell you nothing and will not betray the dacoits. But we notice the smiles of the village people, the way the men preen and twirl their moustaches, the way they walk with a spring in their step. They are proud of their robbers. These small things tell you that the bad boys are in town.'

In the Chambal badlands, I footslogged with police patrols all day. After supper in a police station, I listened to the officers' stories. They reminisced about the life and death of Pan Singh Tomar, an athlete who had represented India and had once held the 3,000 metres record. He killed a man in a quarrel over land and fled to the Chambal ravines to set up as a bandit. Like all dacoits, he and his followers relied on villagers. Pan Singh and his gang went too far. In Pawa village, people showed me the place where the bandits punished the community by taking five men from their homes and shooting them. Some months later, Pan Singh and nine of his followers entered Rathiankapura village. Here they felt secure. It was the home of one of the gang, so they could relax. Pan Singh paid handsomely for a night in a house, a bottle of whisky and a goat to feed his followers. He had a whitewashed room with a simple painting of a tiger. A diligent book keeper, he noted the details of his spending in a blue notebook. He kept a record of the shares he paid to his men after a robbery. Usually the chief took half the spoils and split the rest according to the firepower of each man's weapon. A new automatic earned more than an old rifle.

He felt safe as he ate his meal and sipped his fiery Indian whisky. As he did so, more than 100 policemen, acting on a tip-off, silently surrounded the house. They launched parachute flares into the sky and opened fire. Pan Singh and his men burst out into a storm of bullets. Next morning a great crowd shuffled past the ten sprawled corpses. Vendors arrived to sell soft drinks and spicy snacks, freshly fried on their little stoves. Pan Singh was forty-nine, with twenty murders and fifty kidnappings on his record.

The police were furious when a bandit called Chabiram brazenly held court in a village and even gave a newspaper interview. He soon went too far when he abducted a girl and killed her parents. Until then he had had a reputation for not harming women. The price put on his head was temptingly large, the equivalent of £6,000, and quite enough for someone to betray him. As bandits do, he described himself as a man who fought for justice and robbed only rich people. In the shootout 150 miles south of Delhi, the police killed Chabiram and a dozen of his men. As usual, the bodies were tied to posts, their arms secured behind them, over staves. People arrived in their thousands to see the display.

The notorious Malkhan Singh was one of those who stared for a long time at the photographs in the newspapers. In ten years as a robber and killer, kidnapper and extortionist, he had made big money. He said his prayers at an image of Kali, the goddess of death, every Monday. At the age of thirty-eight, however, he was tired of being on the run, afraid to sleep two nights in the same place. He knew that the police would get him eventually. He reckoned that the game was up. He sent messages to politicians and policemen and negotiated a surrender.

I went to the town of Bhind, in the state of Madhya Pradesh, to witness this extraordinary spectacle. Malkhan topped the wanted lists and styled himself 'Malkhan Singh, Bandit King.' These were the words on his notepaper and ransom demands. 'Bandit King' was also on the rubber stamp he used for his signature.

Thousands of people travelled by bus and ox-cart and on foot to see Malkhan and his men surrender. A ceremonial platform was built, six feet high, shaded by a yellow, green and red awning, and adorned with pictures of Mahatma Gandhi and Pandit Nehru. In carnival style, loudspeakers blared Bollywood film music and songs.

Few people had seen Malkhan before. He paused for photographers as he climbed the steps of the dais, a tall, thin man with the luxuriant moustache that bandits favour. Like many a dacoit leader, he wore a khaki police uniform, a cap and a superintendent's insignia. He carried a dagger, a revolver and a whistle.

On the platform, he held up his rifle with both hands and knelt to place it at the feet of the chief minister of Madhya Pradesh. He made a short speech. No doubt the police thought he would look better with a noose round his neck, but the politicians earned the kudos of ending a criminal's career. Malkhan went to the jail at Gwalior, a city famed for its great rock sculptures on a sandstone hill. He was relieved that he was no longer on the run. 'It's a bad life,' he reflected, 'always being hunted.'

For the newspapers, Phoolan Devi was a welcome phenomenon among dacoit leaders in central India, a woman in charge of men. She made headlines after leading a raid on a riverside village in 1982. Higher caste men had murdered her lover and she had had her revenge. Newspapers reported that, with her Sten gun, she had killed about twenty men in a notorious massacre.

The press called Phoolan 'bandit queen.' After years on the run, she, too, surrendered before a crowd in Bhind, wearing police khaki, her hair tied by a red bandanna. She went through the ritual of placing her rifle at the feet of the chief minister. A film based on her life was a popular success. After eleven years in jail, rather more than she had bargained for, she went into politics and became a member of parliament in Delhi.

In the summer of 1994, I called on her at her neat apartment in the capital. She smiled brightly, talked happily and made tea. I took photographs of her. In 2001 a gunman confronted her at the same apartment door and killed her. He was a member of the Thakur caste, avenging the shooting of 1982. He was arrested and jailed.

In southern India, a bandit called Veerappan murdered more than 100 men as he terrorized his way to control of the profitable trade in the sacred sandalwood tree. He was also a kidnapper who held businessmen to ransom. Roaming the forest east of Mysore, he and his gang killed suspected informers and exhibited their heads in the villages. He taunted the police. He swaggered and grew a magnificent moustache.

His big money came from white sandalwood, prized for its fragrance and burnt as incense in temples. Rendered into a paste it is used to bless and anoint worshippers. No sandalwood tree is privately owned: even if grown on private land, it belongs to the government. It was traditionally used in cremations and is today so rare and expensive that only a few chips of it go onto the pyre. Craftsmen carve it into combs, beads, statuettes of gods and elephants. Its scent lingers for years. Veerappan started his criminal life as an ivory poacher and killed hundreds of elephants before moving into the sandalwood business. He slaughtered his rivals and policemen in gun battles until at last, in 2004, the police trapped and killed him.

Chapter 9

Heaven's river

I saw the parchment skin of a thin old man. His body lay on a worn step facing the Ganges. One of his arms stretched towards the river. Sunlight gleamed on his heels. Hindus believe that death beside the mother river ensures a soul's ascent to heaven. Many who travel to the city of Varanasi hope that it will be their peaceful deathplace.

Indians count seven sacred rivers. The Ganges is mother of them all. It is itself a goddess. It rises in a cave of ice 15,000 feet high in the Himalayas and flows for 1,500 miles into the Bay of Bengal. It crosses the Gangetic Plain, the home of half of India's people.

You may journey to Varanasi a dozen times. You will not forget the first. In the darkness before dawn, feet are pattering. A rustling stream of pilgrims hurries though lanes and labyrinths to the holiest of the river terraces, the Dasaswamedh ghat.

In the gloom, you hear a bustle of rocking boats and a clattering of oars. From a child, you buy a tiny coracle fashioned from a leaf. In it splutters a slender candle. You launch it onto the river to join the flickering toy flotilla. Between the sky and the river, your skiff is a stipple in an ethereal painting. The milky auroral light snuffs the last stars and discloses jumbled outlines of the medieval city. The red sliver of the sun appears. The sound of tambourines and bells accompanies wrapped corpses to the burning ghat.

Along the curving riverbank rise temples and towers, shrines, ashrams, palaces, hotels, tea shops, crammed alleys and crumbling houses. On the river steps, shadowy at first, then pink and gold as the sun ascends, worshippers in hundreds slip into the stream. Busy barbers shave the heads of devout men about to take the waters. In pleasure and piety, they splash and rub and sip and scrub, surfacing rinsed and renewed.

On the hearths of the burning ghats work the servants of the dead, the Doms, the untouchables. They pad catlike among the smoky ashes and prepare fresh logs. Death is the heart of things. Amidst this riverfront life, the vivacity of the living, the blackened cremation grounds are the portals of auspicious despatch to which the dead, with no great solemnity, are briskly brought. They arrive in endless relay, some on rickshaws, others on the roofs of taxis. The river absorbs the ashes of the dead, the animal carcases and sewage. People drink the water and bathe in it, certain of its purity.

Slipping into the shallows, brides pray for fertility. Ganges droplets dripped from a bottle onto soil ensure abundant crops. An oath sworn on the water attests to truth. Refer to a girl as a daughter of the Ganges and you please her parents. Hindus throughout the world yearn to travel to the river at least once in their lives.

Meanwhile, slap-slap at their nearby ghat, washermen thrash trousers and hang them on a rail.

Your boat bumps the steps. No longer peering through morning's misty chiffon, you step ashore, wriggle through the wedding parties, past the shrivelled and the desperate. You are an extra in the opera. Touts tug and peddlers importune. Begging and commerce intertwine. Men play cards; their neighbours pray. A man thumbs vermilion onto my forehead and promises to send a prayer first class to heaven.

Pilgrims' feet have smoothed these steps for 3,000 years. You have joined the centuries. Ralph Fitch, who was here in 1584, was the first Englishman to see Varanasi. His descriptions place you at his side. English Christians who strode through nineteenth-century India, certain that theirs was a superior faith, could not understand how sacredness and smell co-existed. An English cleric of the 1890s, finding 'a loathsome stench' and an 'overgrown fabric of idolatry', admitted that Christian missions had made little impression on Hinduism's 'impenetrable solidity'. Mahatma Gandhi was pained by Varanasi's squalor. The writer, Nirad Chaudhuri, aware of the stink, of the presence of a criminal underworld, of rapacious priests and 'the harlots of Benares', saw beside the Ganges an unforgettable revelation of Hinduism's power.

Varanasi is at the heart of the Hindu universe, a concentrate of gods, temples and humanity. Considering its antiquity and magnificence,

squalor and deformity, you can see why people might despise and
adore it all at once. Varanasi leans on its fabulous history, feeds and
draws strength. It is India. It makes you confront yourself.

★

Every year, in June or July, the great god Jagganath is prepared for his
summer holiday. His brother and sister go with him. The spectacle
is one of the most magnificent of the Hindu festivals. Jagganath is
a monstrous white-faced wooden idol, five feet tall and legless. He
has glaring eyes and short arms, and his head is adorned with a large
diamond. He lives with a black-faced brother and a yellow-faced sister.
Their impish grins and gaudy colouring make them seem almost jolly.

They rule the great temple at Puri, in eastern India, itself one of the
most hallowed of Hindu holy places. A chosen few of the idols' 6,000
servants wash the effigies and brush their teeth. They clothe them in
finery and serve them a breakfast of wheat, sugar and rice. This daily
ritual is at least 1,000 years old. Later the gods have lunch and a siesta.

Meanwhile the city of Puri seethes, hundreds of thousands of
squirming people cramming every street, window, rooftop and
balcony. Cows and bullocks run amok. Uproar enters your bones. Men
jig incessantly to the beat of drums, becoming entranced. Women cut
their hair and bring their tresses in offering. People smash coconuts on
the ground and anoint themselves.

As the multitude roars, the three gods are prepared to ride in great
chariots to their summer house a mile away. Jagganath's vehicle is the
largest, forty-five feet high, mounted on sixteen wheels each seven feet
in diameter. The other two vehicles are only slightly smaller. Thick
ropes are attached to them. More than 4,200 men pull each chariot.

As they lurch forward, the wheels shriek in torment. The chariots are
like terrifying monsters. Drums, horns and cymbals add to the roaring
cascade of noise. Jagganath's name means lord of the universe. Now
we see how the word juggernaut has entered the English language,
meaning an overwhelming force. As night falls, the gods are halfway to
their summer home. The men hauling the chariots are exhausted. Early
in the morning they pick up the ropes. The fantastic noise begins again.

★

Two intrepid artists, Thomas Daniell and his nephew William, were among the first to show the marvels of India to the people of Britain. Their inspiration was William Hodges who had sailed with Captain Cook on his second Pacific exploration in 1772-75 and then painted in India between 1780 and 1783. Thomas Daniell had entered the art world as a painter of scenes on the doors of stagecoaches. He saw hope in the new appetite for oriental pictures and he and William set off in high spirits in 1784. They planned to employ new technology to make aquatints, prints from copper plates.

Their Indian travels included the northern plains and hills, and a long boat trip on the Ganges which brought them to Varanasi, then known as Benares. They painted the pilgrims immersing themselves at the bathing ghats. The success of this northern trip, the rewarding sale of their work, enabled them to fund a tour of southern India, another profitable journey.

After more expeditions, they returned to London with a great store of work. They drew on it for the rest of their lives. To the British public, their paintings and aquatints were compelling distillations of Indian magnificence and romance.

★

Maharaj Dalip Singh, a striking figure with a rakish Rajput moustache, who had restored his home, Fort Chanwa, in Rajasthan, presided over dinner on his veranda. He had a deep knowledge of wars and warriors. He explained to me the importance of opium to the fighting man. 'The ritual use of opium was always widespread in western Rajasthan and eastern Gujarat. It was popular among the warrior classes for four important reasons. One, it was a relaxant that diminished fear before battle. Two, it was a stimulant that worked against fatigue. Three, it was a blood coagulant that helped to heal wounds. Four, it also promoted constipation. A most useful benefit to a warrior riding off to fight, don't you think?'

In the portico of a palace in Madhya Pradesh, a guard stood taut and splendid, his right hand gripping a long spear. He wore a scarlet coat with gold facings and a turban of palest rose. His brambly white beard was fashioned into a fork. He sprang from a tribe of minstrels.

Many years before, he had made it plain to his family that he would work nowhere but at the palace. Any other position was beneath his dignity. As I learned, he had what some men would consider an ideal matrimonial arrangement. He had two wives. One of them cooked, the other did the housework. The only clouds in his life arose when he displeased one or the other of them, as he did occasionally, and they united to throw him out of the house. Whenever this happened, he volunteered for night guard duty at the palace, muttering that there was 'a bit of trouble at home'. When he was forgiven and restored to their affections, his wives gave him a massage, one wife to each leg.

★

Diana Rigg, the actress, and her brother Hugh, returned to the scene of their idyllic childhood in Rajasthan, where their father was a railway superintendent. I joined them on a journey into the Raj. We explored their former home in Bikaner, and drove to the Karniji temple, the home of thousands of sacred rats. We watched great mobs of rats drinking milk and eating food fed to them by priests. They skittered over our bare feet and Diana's red-painted toes. 'I can feel their hard, little droppings under my feet,' she said. As the former Emma Peel of *The Avengers*, she took all that in her stride.

★

Burma, 1981. The country is strikingly beautiful. Emerald paddy fields stretch to blue hills. I fly from Rangoon to Mandalay in a rattling old plane. A lot of the squawking and chattering aboard comes from chickens in their cages. Temples are everywhere: blink and you miss a pagoda. The vistas are of rivers and hills and temples tiled with gold and bright with jewels, filled with images of Buddha, the enduring face of Burma. Buddhism shapes the people. 'It helps us to take life as it comes,' a Burmese explains. 'It will always be the most important part of our lives. The regime has introduced a sense of caution, a looking over the shoulder we did not have before. But we still have our humour.'

Burmese women have a certain dignity. They don't walk behind their men. They look you in the eye. They receive equal pay and, like the men, smoke eight-inch cheroots. Remember Kipling's line in *Mandalay*: 'An' I seed her first a-smokin' of a whackin' white cheroot.' Women also smear sandalwood paste on their faces. It looks like marzipan and is said to be death to pimples.

Street football is played seriously in Rangoon. At critical moments, a referee with a whistle holds up traffic while an attack is completed. People flock to the cinemas. A Burmese girl tells me she likes Western films because they make her cry. 'I like to cry,' she says, 'and I like hearing English.'

Television is new in Burma. It broadcasts for only two hours a day and sets are so expensive that people go to hotels to watch. I discover that the Three Stooges, who made British and American children laugh in the 1950s, are a big hit on television in Burma. Large and lumbering American cars, veterans of the 1940s, are the taxis of Rangoon. Many of the city's buildings are colonial gothic and covered with moss.

The Strand Hotel, where I stay, serves British lunches. Its lost property cupboard in the reception area is full of mildewed razors and single earrings mislaid and left behind forty years before. Few Burmese are allowed to travel abroad, but people are well-informed about the outside world through the BBC, foreign films and the magazines and books sold on the streets. In Rangoon's Golden Pagoda, girls arrive with long switches of their hair and place them on racks, with their names on a card, as offerings to Buddha. Such rituals are commonplace, for this is a country where religion is embedded, monks venerated, and no hamlet is without its pagoda. The people live simply and eat well. Petrol is cheap, the literacy rate high, the black market vigorous.

*

In Sri Lanka, in 1981, I went to a press reception and had a gin and tonic with the Queen and the Duke of Edinburgh. It was a happy royal visit. In some ways, little had changed since the Queen was here in 1954. There was still considerable charm, the shops seemed unchanged since colonial times and there were postcards of the Queen left over from 1954. The pianist at my hotel tinkled melodies from the 1930s and 1940s, radio announcers had a comforting Home Service intonation, the beaches were dazzling white curves and you had Pimm's beneath the palms. On the streets, there were still quite large herds of Morris Minors. During their visit, the Queen and the Duke saw the sacred city of Anuradhapura. She took off her shoes to inspect the sacred bo tree, where Buddha is said to have found enlightenment. The Duke padded in wearing brown socks. The bo custodian wore a cummerbund forty-two yards long.

Legend says Sri Lanka was the original Eden. Alternatively, Arabs called it Serendip, the happiness word. Yet an ugliness was growing, recent rioting and a dozen murders, an aspect of the new 're-ordering' of Sri Lanka's society. The British ruled for 133 years and left in 1948. But a poison was at work and violence became the chief characteristic of Sri Lanka's politics. There were two communities. The Buddhist Sinhalese, 70 per cent of the population, spoke Sinhala. The Tamils, 20 per cent, spoke Tamil. Here was the heart of an acrimonious quarrel.

The British had ruled Ceylon as a single community in which Tamils learned English and prospered. Now that the country was independent, the Sinhalese vowed to replace English with Sinhala, which would be the sole official language. The Tamils, it was argued, could go 'home' to India. This was a divisive and dangerous policy. The Sinhalese had only their island and were determined that it would never be divided. The Tamil Tiger guerrillas were formed by a fanatical leadership. Violence grew out of control into an horrific and ruthless thirty-year war with numerous suicide bombings by the Tigers and mass killing by the army. In my reporting trips to Sri Lanka I would find only a monstrous brew. I grew to know President Jayewardene quite well. He found himself in the worst of times, running out of options. He asked some of us, foreign correspondents, 'Where am I wrong? What would you do?' And as he said farewell he added: 'One thing you haven't told me – how to govern the country in this situation.'

I used to have briefings from a government official. One day he said: 'The history points to the future, and I see only killing, killing, and no more peace.' Suddenly he wept. The horror and waste of it all grew worse.

Chapter 10

Knickerbocker guys

Charles Wilson, who would become editor of *The Times*, invited me to dinner at his home in London. I did not know why. During the meal, the name of Jerry Hall slipped into the conversation and I confessed I did not know who Jerry Hall was. 'Well,' said Charlie, 'how can you be appointed New York correspondent if you don't know who Jerry Hall is?' I was taken aback. Charlie laughed and shook my hand. I said it would be an adventure, and I promised to discover who Jerry Hall was.

Three weeks after leaving Delhi, we were in Manhattan and setting up as Knickerbockers, an old name for New Yorkers. From our predecessor, we inherited a long Ford Thunderbird.

On a sunny morning, a realtor took Penny to look at apartments. A naked man jogged towards them. The realtor beamed. 'That's New York,' he said, as if the city never failed to surprise.

We made our home in an eleventh-floor apartment in East 56th Street. From the top, we could see the East river and, looking south, Manhattan's plantation of towers. According to the medical director of the United Nations, people who could live with New York noise could live anywhere. We were a long distance from Delhi nights. No chowkidars chirruped on East 56th. No tigers yawned. Life in New York seemed at times like a hand-cranked movie, with a night-time thrum of subterranean pistons, a tormenting tinnitus punctuated by the plaintive howl of lonely dogs. We soon absorbed the wailing sirens of the night and the fire brigade's alpenhorns. We bought no earplugs. When we had time, we swam in our tiny lagoon, the soothing rooftop pool. We counted our lengths and saw Manhattan's windows become crosswords at dusk. We agreed that if we could not sleep we would be proper New Yorkers and stroll to the 24-hour Korean grocery to buy mangoes. We never did.

I placed my desk in a corner of our apartment, by the window. It was a small space, but an accountant came to measure it so that we could get a tax allowance. I rose early to scoop up the newspapers outside the door. By six o'clock, eleven o'clock in London, I had read *The New York Times, Wall Street Journal* and *Washington Post*. I had heard the news headlines on radio station WINS. 'You give us 22 minutes, we'll give you the world.'

Then I talked to the foreign desk. Washington reporters wrote the major political and presidency news. My territory included New York itself, the wider coast to coast United States, American life, Canada, the Caribbean and South and Central America. It was a mobile existence. It was easy, at short notice, to fly from JFK and La Guardia. I enjoyed a lunch with Rupert Murdoch at his Manhattan headquarters.

I typed my stories, old-style, but the typewriter age was ending. I first used a computer in 1984, reporting Count Basie's funeral at a church in Harlem. Basie had learned much of his music here, watching Fats Waller play a cinema organ. I wrote up the funeral on a small computer in the back of a taxi, and connected it to my telephone with two large, black rubber cups. For me Basie's *One O'Clock Jump* signalled the new age in newspapers.

Settling into the neighbourhood we tried out the restaurants. A waiter schooled us in Manhattan manners. 'My name is Leopold,' he said, fairly heavily, 'and I am your waiter this evening. I can tell from your accents that you folks are British. You may not know that here in New York customers tip fifteen per cent.' He paused and said: 'Minimum.'

In this great alimentary city, a meal could be a drama. The caste system in some restaurants divided clients into divines and peasants. We read that a celebrated New York restaurant critic quit her job, felled by obesity, unable to leave anything on her plate.

We discovered a blessing, that our apartment was within the orbit of the goddess Greta Garbo, loveliest of enigmas. She had retired at the age of thirty-five and lived in seclusion nearby. She might be glimpsed occasionally wearing a sheltering hat and dark glasses. Mr Socrates, a grocer, said that local people respected Miss Garbo's privacy. More than that, they enjoyed the reflected light. They were proud and protective.

Greta Garbo weakened the knees of a generation of men. What about that scene where she placed her lips on the communion cup where her lover had planted his? What about the time when she drew her lover's bouquet close to her body? What about 'Gif me a visky, ginger ale on the side,' her first soundtrack words in *Anna Christie*? A movie critic said that her voice was revealed as 'a deep, husky, throaty contralto that possesses every bit of that fabulous poetic glamour that has made this distant Swedish lady the outstanding actress of the motion picture world'. After seeing *Flesh and the Devil* in 1926, a critic wrote that there were three love scenes in it 'that will make hair rise on end, an' that ain't all. This girl has everything'.

Miss Garbo's elegant home overlooked a sculpture garden and the swirling East river. By her pool, in her sixties, she taught her niece's children how to perform cartwheels. She summered in Switzerland. A florist said to me that it was 'an honour to have her living here'. A bookseller confided: 'Sometimes she comes in and we chat a little. She is still lovely, you know.' He recalled a sweet moment when she tilted her head back, 'just as she did in the famous photograph. Time stood still'. A meat shop manager said that Miss Garbo was a vegetarian, but came in when she had guests. 'She smiles at us through the window, a shy and gracious lady, and then there's that unmistakable voice.' A shop assistant thought Miss Garbo was 'really rather wonderful. She doesn't say much when she comes in, but she smiles. She's nearly eighty and the beauty is still there'.

An American reporter I knew was a trencherman. His contact book bulged with restaurant numbers. He called to say: 'I heard you were heading for Florida. Don't miss Joe's Stone Crab in Miami. Don't even think of going anywhere else.' In Washington he said: 'Tonight, I'll take you to the top pizza place in town.' As we sat at the table, he ordered a large pizza for us to share, something to fill the hungry gap while we studied the menu.

Another American reporter of my acquaintance lived in Florida. 'Call me when you're in Miami,' he urged. I did. 'Where are staying?' he said. I told him. He gasped. 'You can't do that. You won't get respect. *The Times* is a top paper. Your editor won't thank you for checking in to a nowhere hotel.'

I checked out of nowhere and upgraded to respect. I found I was two inches taller. My American colleague beamed approval when we met.

I embraced the excitement of Cape Canaveral and the space coast towns. Here, I imagined, astronauts dropped in for steaks after all that moonwork. I wrote the story of Sally Ride, who had answered an Astronauts Wanted newspaper ad. She had the right stuff to be the first American woman in space, thirty-two years old, thumbnailed in the papers as Cool Hand Sally, more laconic than a Spartan, as awshucks as Gary Cooper. 'She has country-boy horse sense,' said her captain, himself a man of few words. 'I like people who don't get too excited.' Nasa's comprehensive briefings left no detail unrecorded. There was barely any gender difference in the space kit, just 'brassiere, female only,' and 'lipstick, female unique'.

On blast-off day in June 1983, the neon signs along the space coast roads shouted 'Ride, Sally, Ride!' From my press seat, I looked beyond lagoons to the launch altar. The space shuttle itself seemed to embrace the monstrous fuel tank. It looked like a bear cub clutching the breast of a mother grizzly. An avuncular voice counted down the minutes. Incandescent light preceded volcanic roar. Earth shook, air crackled, birds fled. All eyes lifted. I looked around. Tears rolled down faces, winking and shining in the rocket flame dazzle.

I drove out of Miami along the Tamiami Trail and became absorbed into the drowsy Florida Everglades. I gazed at an immense body of shallow and shining water moving over 5,000 square miles of marshland, of mangrove forests and tangled creeks. I travelled all the way to the mazy Ten Thousand Islands in the Floridian south-west. Somewhere, as I strolled in the exotic Everglades, I turned a corner on a wooden walkway and came face to jaws with a sunbathing alligator. In an instant I jumped back on sprung heels. The beast itself flopped into the water. We both had a fright. Alligators may occasionally kill a human, but they prefer those small and crunchy lapdogs. Perhaps we can see them as representatives of the opportunist spirit of Florida business.

In the 1920s land rush, two million suckers invested in Floridian dream land that in reality lay under water. By 1926, even the banks thought better of building on water. Some businessmen tried to keep out hurricane relief teams, believing that publicity would shrink the value of property in paradise.

Al Capone, the Illinois alligator, slithered into Miami and died there in 1947. More gangsters came and moved into racket management. In the golden fifties age of war-generated prosperity, Florida was a wide-open frontier. When Castro took power in Cuba, and a large part of the Cuban middle class fled to Florida, Miami grew rich on new brainpower and acumen. Within twenty years, Miami had 200 Cuban millionaires.

For many years, the aquatic Everglades were considered fit only for drainage and development. It was Marjory Stoneman Douglas who saved them from such ignorance. She had the power of her pen, composing with rhythmic clarity the classic book of Florida's waterlands, *The Everglades: River of Grass*. 'There are no other Everglades in the world,' she began. 'Nothing anywhere else is like them.' Published in 1947, the book still sells thousands of copies. The case she made for the Everglades was simple: if businessmen or politicians destroyed them, Florida itself would rapidly become desert.

She invited me to tea at her one-room, book-buttressed home in Coconut Grove on the edge of Miami. She liked to write on the veranda overlooking her garden. She was then almost 100 years old. She first lived in Miami in 1915 when its population was 5,000. Her father founded the *Miami Herald* and employed her as a journalist. She was a Red Cross nurse during the first world war, serving in Belgium, Italy and the Balkans. After the war, she was the *Herald*'s assistant editor. She never got round to learning to drive. She was a delightful interviewee. She didn't forget to tell me, as she told others, that she drank a glass of whisky at five o'clock every afternoon. She didn't really like the taste, she added, 'but I don't know anything else that does what it does for me'. She was 108 when she died.

*

In October 1983, President Reagan sent American troops to Grenada to rescue the island people from Cuban and rebel Grenadian forces. The popular Grenadian Marxist leader, Maurice Bishop, and five friends, had been put against a wall and shot by his Grenadian enemies. Most Grenadians hated the coup leaders and welcomed the Americans. I arrived from Barbados in an American military plane. 'We had a good old fight,' an American officer said, bringing me up to date, 'just like the old days.' Fighting was still going on. A house recently taken by American troops was bloody from floor to ceiling. The foot of a Grenadian soldier poked from a shallow grave. Snipers were still active. No phones were working in the island. I found space in an American plane that evening and shuttled to Barbados to send my reports to London. I flew back at daybreak, then back and forth for several days. As it turned out, the American intervention in Grenada was welcome and successful.

★

I flew to Buenos Aires in January 1984. Day by day, the crimes of Argentina's military regime were emerging in shocking detail. The junta was steeped in crime and cruelty. These men ruled for eight years and sent thousands of their countrymen to their deaths. More than 7,000 victims had been registered as desaparecidos, disappeared ones. One estimate put the death toll at 30,000. I learned that death squads had cut off the hands of many murdered people to prevent identification. Television pictures showed the exhumations. Of 482 bodies found buried in one town, 229 were of people shot in the head. Others were strangled or burned. Many victims were thrown alive from aircraft. Reports said that death squads had killed children of five.

Jacobo Timerman, a Jewish writer and newspaper editor, was jailed and tortured by the junta for thirty months. He was fortunate to escape the army's death squads and went to Israel. He wrote a book about his ordeal: *Prisoner Without a Name, Cell Without a Number.* I interviewed him in Buenos Aires when he made a return visit to Argentina. 'I lived and worked in this city for most of my life,' he told me, 'but somehow the streets and buildings do not look the way they used to look. So much brings back memories of torture. I don't want to kill the torturers, I want them to face justice. What a strange country. We had everything but we destroyed it.'

I was moved by the steadfast Mothers of the Plaza de Mayo, quietly courageous women who, for eight years, had met every Thursday afternoon to walk in the city square in silent demonstration. They wore scarves bearing the names of their missing children. Like water dripping on a stone their brave protest eventually helped to break the detested generals. At the military barracks, a uniform had become an object of contempt, not of pride. The police were despised. An archbishop was sacked for supporting military leaders with spiritual counsel. Shops dared to put up signs saying: Welcome Democracy. In a time of runaway inflation, I had the weird experience of paying for a £3 lunch with a million-peso note.

I flew from Buenos Aires to Trelew in Patagonia. The newspaper I bought at the airport reported the unearthing of the bones of twenty people from Trelew district who had disappeared during the junta's rule. I took a taxi to Gaiman in the Chubut Valley. A boisterous wind bowled great balls of dust through the town. On this hot Sunday afternoon, the town's main street was wide and empty, like the street in *High Noon* before the showdown. I saw a man inventing a zoo, cutting animal shapes from sheets of tin and planting them in his garden. He was painting the stripes on a zebra while a yellow and black tin tiger dried in the sun.

He directed me to the home of Handel and Glenys Jones who were entertaining their cousin, Gweno Rees de Jones. They were all jolly. In my honour, Glenys took the curlers from her hair and put on a new pinafore made in Wales. As we patched a conversation in Spanish, Welsh and a little English, they insisted I had a proper Welsh tea of bread and butter, scones, jam, cream and cake. They thought it strange that I refused milk and sugar in my tea and looked into my cup saying: 'Dim llaeth, dim siwgr, fancy.' I went to crowded Puerto Madryn and saw the striking monument marking the place where 153 Welsh pioneers landed in 1865 and founded their colony, a remarkable little chapter in man's pursuit of dreams.

Like many Argentines the people of Patagonia did not find it easy to talk of the Falklands war of 1982 or the repression. They learned the habit of reticence under military rule and tended to look at their shoes when the subject arose. 'I had an unspoken agreement with my

Argentine friends in the war,' a rancher told me. 'We did not talk about it.'

I flew from Trelew to Esquel in western Patagonia and stayed at Mrs Rowlands's guest house. She gave me a large tea of scones and cream and in the morning a breakfast of sausages and eggs. At the bus station, there was a small crowd of gauchos in low black hats and baggy trousers, looking as bereft as the habitually mounted always do when horseless. I found a bus going my way, to Trevelin. I had been invited to lunch in Esquel with a farmer and his wife. Late in the afternoon I flew back to Buenos Aires.

★

I went to Canada to report Mrs Thatcher's talks with Pierre Trudeau, the prime minister. She was said to have described his attitude to the Soviet Union as 'wet'. She enjoyed making a speech to parliament, saying 'We do not want peace at any price. Tyrants do not tackle those who are strong.' Summarizing her day, I wrote that she ate a television journalist for breakfast and bit off the heads of two reporters at a press conference. 'Aren't you used to directness?' she challenged the scribblers. 'It comes as second nature to me.'

★

News seeping from Haiti promised trouble. I flew to Port-au-Prince and checked into a balcony room at Oloffson's, a dowager witness to Haiti's long misrule. It had been a hotel since the 1930s, a picture of white fretwork, gingerbread gables, turrets and verandas. The palms and Victorian style suggest theatre scenery. A newspaper report from Haiti lacking a sentence of Graham Greene's description of Oloffson's in *The Comedians* seemed somehow incomplete.

I drove from Port-au-Prince to a nearby seaside town and found 2,000 angry people demonstrating against Jean-Claude Duvalier, their brutal and thieving ruler. Summoned by church bells and drums, they carried a coffin as a symbol of protest. They showed me the bodies of two people shot by the president's sinister police.

Sacred water: women bathing in the Ganges at Varanasi

Gun, knife, dagger, whistle and big moustache: the bandit king surrenders

Phoolan Devi, bandit queen and Member of Parliament at home in Delhi

Afghanistan. Dawn discloses majestic mountain beauty, a sparkling river and curving canyon

The long walk to Tora Bora: the author reaches the mountain stronghold of the mujahidin fighters

Off to fight the Russians: Pathans in the Afghan mountains

Burma's sublime pagodas: elegant architecture grew from religious fervour

'Something to live for' – cowboy prisoners at jail rodeo, Huntsville, Texas

Kyoto, Japan: a yawn of Buddhist schoolboys

India's republic day spectacular: bagpipes and bonnets …

… and the measured majesty of noble elephants

Alaska: the grandeur of mountains

At Luxor, on the bank of the Nile, a face of ancient Egypt

The Duvaliers, father and son, Papa Doc and Baby Doc, had ruled Haiti's five million people with great cruelty since 1957. Papa Doc, who died in 1971, recruited the notorious death squads called the Tontons Macoutes after the fictional bogeyman who stuffed children into a bag. Thousands of Tontons formed a paramilitary force wielding guns and machetes. As killers and looters they drew no pay, but simply helped themselves to money, food and property.

Baby Doc was a fat and lazy playboy of nineteen when he became president for life. He had no appetite for the office. He and his wife Michele married in 1980 and stole their country's revenue, the foreign aid. She shopped in New York and Paris for furs. For all its crippling poverty, Haiti boasted a Club Méditerranée.

Early in 1986, the Reagan government was ready to expel the Duvaliers. With some courage businessmen shut their shops and offices and called for democracy. I saw Baby Doc in Port-au-Prince making a rare public appearance to claim that he still ruled. His jewelled wife drove him around the capital. He even got out of the car to assert that his grip on Haiti was 'as firm as a monkey's tail'. Tontons Macoutes, sinister in sunglasses, strode the streets brandishing guns and exuding menace. For all that, Baby Doc was clearly on the way out and Port-au-Prince sizzled with rumour.

That evening some of us went to a voodoo ceremony. Voodoo is Haiti's folk religion, a solace, part of the struggle against evil. As people danced the beating of drums accelerated to a frenzy. A man stepped forward, his skin glistening, and in that frantic moment he grasped a struggling chicken. He appeared to bite off its head in a shower of blood.

Back in the city, we heard that Baby Doc and his family would fly into exile within a few hours. Reporters and photographers gathered at Duvalier airport. At midnight, the Duvaliers hosted a champagne party for their cronies. At two o'clock an American C-141 cargo plane landed, a flying pantechnicon. Such was the tension that a couple of television cameramen traded punches, jostling for a prime place to film. After three o'clock a convoy of cars arrived, heavy with Gucci and Louis Vuitton luggage.

Baby Doc was a sullen figure at the wheel of his Mercedes as he

97

drove to the plane's ramp. His nose-in-the-air wife was haughty by his side. She wore a white dress and puffed a cigarette, smiling through the camera flash. More than twenty of the family and bodyguards went aboard for the flight to France. It was time to file the story to London.

As the plane took off we saw the slight figure of Aubelin Jolicoeur, a regular at Oloffson's bar, a dapper dresser with a silver-topped cane. In *The Comedians*, Graham Greene had cast him as Petit Pierre, a journalist always consulted by visiting reporters. He had come to see the ending of the Duvalier story.

At Oloffson's a phone was working. There were still drinks. A French reporter was at the piano extemporizing a jazzy ditty:

> Pack up your suits, Macoutes,
> We've found your loot, Macoutes,
> Get on your route, Macoutes,
> You've got the boot, Macoutes,
> Toot, toot, toot, toot Macoutes.

In the morning, the Haiti newspapers were, for the first time, full of real news. With the tyrant gone, a crowd hurried in the early light to Papa Doc's tomb in the cemetery. They were out to desecrate his bones. But the tomb was empty. Perhaps Baby Doc had foreseen what might happen. Determined on some sort of vengeance, the crowds opened the grave of one of Papa Doc's henchmen and stoned the bones. For the time being, the Tontons Macoutes were on the run.

★

I was in Canada in March 1984 when Pierre Trudeau resigned. 'A lot of us hated him, a lot of us liked him, too,' a young woman said. 'We'll miss him because he made us come alive. He got us by the scruff of the neck and shook us. For all his faults, he made us more aware of our country. That's what we'll thank him for.' Trudeau was enigmatic. He lived for the day and did not look too far ahead. With one short break, he had been Liberal prime minister for sixteen years and knew that Canada ached for a change. He instinctively cut against the grain, an intellectual French-Canadian, impulsive, arrogant, charismatic, a devoted flouter of convention and possessor of one of the phenomenal egos of modern politics.

★

'Mine honour,' says the Duke of Norfolk in *Richard II,* 'is my life.' With this in mind, two famous generals fought for honour's sake in a gripping double bill at the federal courthouse in Manhattan.

In courtroom 318, I heard the scratching of charcoal on sketch pads as newspaper artists defined the jutting jaw of General William Westmoreland. Every day his wife sat in court and listened to the evidence, her hands busy with her needlework.

The general said he was 'lynched' on a television programme. His lawyer said: 'It is a matter of a soldier's honour. Those guys called him a liar. If this had happened in England they would have been drawn and quartered.'

Two floors below, in another court, the Israeli General Ariel Sharon fought *Time* magazine, citing a 'blood libel'. Both generals were suing for immense sums of money: more than £100 million in the case of General Westmoreland, aged seventy, and £45 million for General Sharon, aged fifty.

Westmoreland was a hero to many Americans, a symbol of a bad war to others. His case drew deeply on the well of bitterness left by defeat in the Vietnam war in which 58,000 Americans died. General Sharon claimed that *Time* magazine published a slur on himself, the Jews and Israel, in writing that he condoned the massacre of 700 Palestinians. After months in court, General Sharon lost his case. General Westmoreland dropped his libel suit. His opponents thought he was trying to rewrite history.

★

Charles Dickens, the master coiner of apt names for his characters, might have found a use for Trump, given its resonance of success and triumph. The new Trump Tower on Fifth Avenue oozed extravagance.

Donald Trump himself noted that New York was becoming a city for the rich, adding that 'wealth and an indefinable "it" would secure good tables in restaurants'. High above the avenue, Trumpian trumpeters in the Trump Tower blew fanfares, a nubile choir sang, a waterfall cascaded, as if scripted by Hollywood.

The pianist Liberace stayed at the tower when he marked his fortieth year as an entertainer. He filled Radio City Music Hall every night for two weeks. The theatre seemed large enough to stable a Zeppelin. I went to report the event. A chauffeur drove a silver Rolls-Royce onto the stage and Liberace alighted in a silver-sequinned suit, trailing a jewelled blue fox cloak sixteen feet long. He and the 6,000 audience members exuded love for each other. He showed off his gold and diamond rings to the front seats. Projected pictures of them made the entire audience gasp.

One of the last of the great solo American performers, Liberace played pieces by Rachmaninov, Chopin, Liszt and Tchaikovsky and appeared in numerous coruscating suits. From time to time he left the stage to slip into something more expensive and returned whirling and flashing like a mirrored ball.

During his absences, the Rockettes, fifty long-limbed dancers and a New York institution, performed their high kicks. In the guise of a Venetian courtier, Liberace played as the piano revolved, coloured fountains danced, an orchestra rose from the bowels of the theatre, waltzers swirled to Strauss.

Liberace exited briefly to take on more jewels, the Rolls-Royce came and he stood in the back of it, his face lit by joy, his shimmering hands outstretched to bless the grateful multitude. Cecil Beaton, who saw a Radio City show in the 1930s, described it as 'one of the best popular entertainments in New York, where the poor man can enjoy himself as much as the millionaire'.

★

Following the long American presidential election campaign, travelling and listening to what people say, is a good education. Ronald Reagan's staff saw to it that, despite his well-known gaffes, the president was always steered into a flattering limelight. 'When you're running for president you do what you are good at,' said Lyn Nofziger, a Reagan aide for many years. 'Ronald Reagan is very good on television. Obviously we run the campaign on television and we restrict his contact with the press. Of course we do. We don't want him to screw up.'

Some of his staff knew Mr Reagan as The Talent, a tribute to his performance skill. They ensured that he was shown in the most favourable way. He was both projected and gagged. He dealt in good news and the evocation of a hopeful America painted by Norman Rockwell.

He did not give good interviews. 'He simply does not have a lot to say,' a political columnist noted. 'I've talked with him privately and he is the same off the record as on. There's nothing deceptive about him. He's a nice man with simple goals.'

This simplicity made Reagan easier to present to the people. He distanced himself from government. The buck did not stop at his desk. Others had taken the heat. Through Ronald Reagan, Americans enjoyed a kind of restoration. When I asked a woman from Nevada about Mr Reagan, she thought for a few seconds and said: 'It's not a bad thing we have an actor for president. Only an actor knows how a president should behave.'

President Reagan went down to Disney World in Florida and shook hands with Mickey Mouse. Minnie Mouse gave him a kiss. But later there was an extraordinary incident at Disney World. The newspapers ran the headline: *Boy, 6, mugged by Mickey Mouse.*

Bizarreries are commonplace in newspapers here, for there is always something amazing happening in America. But even with a newspaper diet of surprises, the eyebrow arched at the Mickey Mouse story.

M. Mouse, it seems, was doing his job, wagging his big ears, posing for photographs, being amiable in keeping with the Disney World atmosphere. Without warning, Boy, 6, tweaked his tail. Well, even Mickey Mouse can have a bad day, and for some reason his agreeable disposition crumbled. Instead of a gentle admonishment with a 'Hey there, li'l feller, don't pull old Mickey's tail now,' he picked up Boy, 6, and threw him at a wall. The lad was undoubtedly surprised, but not badly hurt.

Everyone agrees that boy-throwing is to be frowned on. The parents are taking Mickey Mouse to court for assault. So this is a bad business. Parents do not take their children to Florida to have them thrown about by Mickey Mice who are not having a nice day.

★

During the night of 2 December 1984, a yellow cloud of poisonous gas leaked from the American Union Carbide plant in the Indian city of Bhopal 300 miles south of Delhi. It killed more than 3,000 men, women and children. The plant had limited protection. It was not in good order. A leak was bound to lead to mass death. Around 100,000 people inhaled the gas, 4,000 were severely injured. I flew from New York to Delhi, arrived early in the morning and spent the day in Bhopal talking to survivors and doctors. Many thousands of people were walking out of the city, afraid to stay. A relentless procession snaked across the pink rock landscape. The building of such a badly-maintained plant, with its deadly chemicals so close to a crammed city, was a fatal error. Most of the people who worked there knew nothing of its dangerous state. They lived in shacks with rudimentary hygiene. Many choked and died in their sleep. Others, who fled, were overtaken by the fatal cloud.

Communications in Bhopal were bad, no telephones working. I flew to Delhi that evening to transmit the story. In a hotel, I encountered Melvin Belli, a flamboyant American lawyer, a bulky figure in a black suit and alligator-skin boots. He said he had arrived to fight for 'the nobodies, some poor little bastard who finds his wife and child dead'. The American businessman, he declared, 'is cruel and unethical, the son of a bitch. We will try to get the case heard in California. I know my juries there and I like my judges. It is my home.' He added, rather oddly: 'When you get to seventy-seven and have two Italian greyhounds and have read as many books as I have, you don't have to spend time justifying yourself.' Mr Belli's companion was a lawyer wearing a baseball cap inscribed with the words Justice Bhopal.

★

British reporters are sometimes surprised that the activities of the mayor of New York are significant news. Civic affairs and local politics create headlines. I note that Ed Koch seeks a third four-year term in office. He is mayor, prime minister and foreign minister and wants to be mayor of New York forever because, he says, it's the best job in the world's greatest city. Fiorello La Guardia, mayor from 1934-45, is often rated as greatest mayor. Ed Koch wants to be judged greater.

I talk to him several times. He fits me into his high-speed schedule, genially invites me to a bigwig party on a big boat. In city hall, he sits at La Guardia's desk. Like La Guardia, he is a natural newsmaker. His mobile features, lifted eyebrows, staccato delivery and shiny pate form a New York landmark. When he opens his mouth the press corps microphones are thrust at him like assegais. He appears on television most days. He is a talker in the New York cabbie tradition, quick on the draw with instant opinions. He often utters words like Outrageous! Baloney! and Schmuck! He likes to get his retaliation in first. He's a boss figure, a tough guy running the show. He is always on the front page. Of course he is. That's where New Yorkers feel they belong.

★

Texans agree that there are no people quite like them. The place names of Texas form a poem: Ike, Fred, Tarzan, Gasoline, Grit, Pep, Teacup, Bug Tussle, Ogg, Roundup, Gun Barrel City, Jot 'Em Down and Gunsight. I bought boots in a store with a large portrait of John Wayne. 'He was, and is, a hero,' the manager said. A rancher invited me to stay at his home. First, though, he called in one of his cowpokes to deal with a rattlesnake on the veranda. The cowpoke killed the snake and reaped his reward in selling the rattle, skin and meat. The rancher poured us both a large Scotch to sip as we headed to a barbecue. 'If you don't mind,' he said, 'I'll take the country road. I won't drive through town holding a whisky. The sheriff's a good friend of mine and I don't want to embarrass him.'

I went to a rodeo at the Crossbar Hotel, prison slang for Huntsville Jail in Texas. Only well-behaved prisoners were permitted to risk their necks in the Huntsville rodeo. They wore black and white striped shirts and trousers, batwing chaps and, of course, cowboy hats. The bulls and bucking broncos were the real thing: it was certainly a dangerous sport.

Most of the cowboys lasted only a few seconds before they were flung into the dust like rag dolls. Forty of them competed for the $400 stuffed into a tobacco pouch. The pouch was tied to the horns of a snorting bull. Most of the cowboys were chased away or thrown high in the air by the angry bull. But one wiry and plucky man grabbed the purse from the horns, ran for his life and kept the prize.

I asked one of the cowboys why he was in jail. 'Had a money-hungry girlfriend,' he said, 'so I got desperate and tried to rob me a bank.' He gave a rueful smile. 'Warn't like it is in the movies, though. So now you see where I am. But I've kept my nose clean and hope to be gettin' into the free world in a few months.' Stanley Stillsmoking, a Blackfoot Indian completing a sentence for burglary, said the rodeo gave men pride and self-respect. The prison chaplain, who was part of our conversation, agreed with him.

Richard Love became a sheriff in west Texas because his predecessor was jailed for five years for drug dealing. 'The whole town was dishonoured,' he told me. 'The sheriff was selling drugs out of the county jail. We looked a bunch of crooks. When I was young, the sheriff was the town kingpin, well-respected. I wanted to wipe out the shame.'

He was a towering figure, 6ft 2in, eighteen stone, lizard skin boots, a Colt with a decorated silver and enamel handle, a gun belt over his trouser belt, big hands, cigarettes in the pocket of his white shirt, the whole eminence crowned by the dove grey Stetson hat marketed as the Texas Sheriff edition.

When I met him, he was the law in Hudspeth County, West Texas, 5,000 square miles of cactus, rattlesnake and canyon country, where the brown Rio Grande forms the Mexico border. Smuggler country, too. In the jail car park were thirty vehicles seized from smugglers.

Sheriff Love requalifies as a marksman every year. He shoots as well with his left hand as his right. A marine in the second world war and the Korean war, he has had his fill of shooting. 'I say a prayer every day, hoping I don't have to use a gun. I've shot at vehicles, not people. As a lawman, I'm supposed to apprehend people, not kill them.'

He showed me round his twenty-cell jail in Sierra Blanca, the county seat ninety miles east of El Paso. 'Sometimes I get hit by a prisoner, but I never hit back. I do put them on the ground pretty fast, something I learned in the Marines. With my height and weight, they stay down. But I always try to treat 'em humanely. You do more with sugar than with salt.'

Every year he takes a school party around his jail. He believes it satisfies curiosity and has a salutary effect.

The sheriff starts his day at 7.30, drinking coffee and smoking cigarettes at a restaurant in Sierra Blanca. This is Texas and men wear their hats all the time they are awake. He holds court and listens to the latest news of drug smuggling and arrests. He has a jail lunch of hamburger steak and mashed potato. Later in the day he drops into a café at Fort Hancock. 'It's important that people see me around a lot.'

Back on the road many cars sped by, over the limit. 'Never given a speeding ticket in my life,' said Love. 'I'm a sheriff, not a speed cop. Reckless drivers – I give them a talking to, not a ticket.' We drove in the daylight's embers. The sheriff, speaking in fluent Texan, called it 'a cowboy sunset'.

In Texas to write about the presidential contest between George Bush Senior and Bill Clinton in 1992, I went in search of Bubba, the authentic Texan. I may have glimpsed him in Houston, dancing the Texas two-step, his belly buttressed by a fist-sized buckle. Now and then I saw him on the road, the quintessential working man, raised in Texas soil, blue-collared and red-necked. He chewed tobacco and tossed beer cans from his pick-up truck, the Texas national vehicle. He seemed to have worn boots and jeans almost from babyhood. His crown was a western hat or a peaked cap advertising a seed company, a popular beer, or a favourite pesticide.

At the bar, he drank Lone Star beer from a longnecked bottle. He listened to any music provided it was country and western. The women he favoured wore halter-tops and turquoise jewellery.

Some Bubbas competed in rodeos, but mostly they watched football on television. A good number of them went dancing with a partner who followed fashion and tucked her left thumb into the belt loop of his jeans. In a traditional hoot-and-holler hall I observed the steps of a

Bubba dance: jiggle your left leg, jiggle your right, kick out your right foot and shout 'Bullshit.'

Many a Bubba took his vacations in Texas since there was nowhere else worth seeing. The Lone Star flag flew everywhere in this vast state. It was printed on T-shirts with the simple legend: Home. In Bubba country, Western clothing stores abound and, yes, that's John Wayne's photo portrait on the wall. Texas boots are made from the skins of calves, goats, alligators, anteaters, kangaroo and ostrich. You would look a picture in crocodile boots trimmed with ermine.

A Texas editor told me that Bubba was real, but also part of Texas myth. He might appear to be a coarse pig-headed reactionary, but he represented a certain Texan individuality. As Texas became more urbanized the real Bubba was disappearing, replaced by weekend suburban Bubbas, pick-up and all, but wearing the wrong jeans and listening to rock and roll instead of country. Until Ronald Reagan came along, many a Bubba voted Democrat. On the other hand loyal Bubbas continued to vote Democrat because their daddy did. I found genuine Bubbas in a bar in Austin listening to a jukebox number called *Gonna Pack Up My Suitcase and Move to the Outskirts of Town.* The bumper stickers on the pick-ups outside, however, struck a sturdy Texan note: It's Hard To Be Humble When You're So Great.

Farther west I watched seven whistling Texas cowboys work their horses to and fro, driving cattle into a corral, painstakingly separating calves from their mothers, sexing, de-horning, inoculating and branding them, castrating the bull calves. When they finished, the cowboys grilled the testes on the branding furnace and popped them, like marshmallows, into their mouths. They gave me one, too. I was watching a dying breed at work. Ranchers said the numbers of skilled hands were dwindling, the quality of horsemanship in decline. 'You have to be special to be a cowboy,' one of them said, 'and our talent pool is drying up.' Still, I met a cowboy happy in his work. 'The job I always wanted,' he said. 'My boy, Casey, two years old, already has his own boots, spurs and rope. He'll be a cowboy, too. In Texas there will always be cowboys.'

★

In Miami in November 1985, I heard news of Colombia's worst natural disaster. The eruption of Nevado del Ruiz volcano swamped the landscape with mud and triggered great avalanches and roaring torrents thick with bodies. More than 25,000 people died. The volcano was a favourite picture postcard, its emerald green slopes topped with a snowcap. I flew to Bogotá and made my way to the town of Armero. It had ceased to exist. It was an island of death.

Everywhere I looked, houses were smashed to matchwood. Hundreds of strewn bodies lay coated in mud like clay statues. A sulphurous ash filled the air. A race was on to find survivors. Rescuers struggled to extract people buried to the neck in mud, trapped and weak, but still alive. It was desperate and harrowing work. I flew in an RAF Puma helicopter delivering supplies of food and medicine to places difficult to reach. Radio stations broadcast the names of the dead in an endless litany. People stood in long lines to give blood.

★

Within minutes of lift-off at Cape Canaveral in 1986 the space shuttle Challenger blew up. All America grieved, stunned by the terrible public death of heroes. This is a tragedy in the family. Many bars around here have space age names and signed photographs of astronauts. People are used to the excitement and thunder of lift-off. Shopkeepers put breezy thumbs-up messages on the boards. The shuttle venture began in 1981, and America grew accustomed to success. The space programme had a social and political role as well as a scientific one. The shuttles carried the first American woman, the first black astronaut, the first Hispanic. President Reagan said the first private citizen in space would be a teacher. Eleven thousand people applied and Christa McAuliffe was selected. She was personable and committed, thirty-seven years old, mother of children aged nine and six. Her parents, husband and children were all in the guest grandstand at Cape Canaveral. People were used to seeing the rocket's white plume of vapour spiralling into the sky like a rope into the heavens. This time the rope seemed to snap and smudged the sky, slowly evaporating. All through the day and night the outdoor digital clock counted the hours, minutes and seconds into the mission that ended almost as soon as it began.

★

I saw John Gotti only once. Danger gleamed in his dark-eyed gaze. He was a gangster of the old school, a looming man, the mafia godfather in New York and therefore the mafia godfather of America, powerful and wealthy. I have not forgotten his stare.

He was not at all a shadowy gangster. He liked to be recognized on the street, the boss of bosses. He enjoyed eating well in good restaurants. He was happy to cut a figure with his close-at-hand bodyguards. His cover story was that he sold plumbing equipment. But crime paid him millions of dollars. As Al Capone said: 'Once in the racket, you're always in it.'

John Gotti liked admiration. Because his Italian suits were so finely tailored, his silk ties so expensive, his coats so superb, people saluted him as the Dapper Don. He kept gentlemen's hours and started every day sitting in a barber's chair to have his silver hair trimmed just so. Once, entering a courthouse, he growled to the jostling photographers. 'You guys,' he said warningly, 'cut it out.' He gallantly stepped to open the door for a woman reporter and said to the photographers: 'I was brought up to hold doors for ladies.' As for the male reporters, he turned to his lawyer and said: 'They get a kick out of playing kids' games.'

At that time the FBI was leaning hard on the five major mafia families of New York: Gambino, Colombo, Bonnano, Genovese and Lucchese. These were an affront to American society. In 1984 an FBI officer said: 'The finely- manicured hands of the Colombo family are at every construction site in New York. You can't pour concrete in this city without paying off the Colombos.' The gangs had commanding influence in drugs, gambling, prostitution and the looting of banks.

Their ultimate sanction was, as always, murder. Describing a mafia prince, a police officer said: 'He gives that look like he might rip your jugular out.' The prince's enemies got him in the end. He was found in a sack, a bullet hole behind each ear.

John Gotti was rising stock in the Gambino family, a tough underworld figure jailed several times as he climbed the crime ladder. Bribery enabled him to spend hours enjoying discreet trips from jail, chauffered to New York restaurants.

At the end of 1985 I covered the murder of the Gambino family boss and a bodyguard outside Sparks steak house on East 46th Street in Manhattan. The police briefly uncovered the bodies for the photographers. 'Only in New York,' said the taxi drivers, shaking their heads. RUBOUT shouted a newspaper headline. Such notoriety drew so many diners that for months you could not get a table at Sparks.

After the murder, John Gotti became the new Gambino godfather. It was in the following year that I saw him in the courthouse wearing an expensive grey Italian suit, a tie and the most elegant camelhair coat you have ever seen. I was in the press seats. He came in and gave me a look that would have drilled holes. He was acquitted. He was finally jailed in 1992 and died in prison in 2002.

A detective once observed that crime families enjoyed gathering to watch *The Godfather* films. They had seen them many times, underworld life imitating art. He told the story of a mafioso under surveillance, who, lunching alone in a restaurant, called the waiter. He gave him a fistful of dollars, instructing him to play *The Godfather* theme on the jukebox. Over and over.

Chapter 11

The syllables of Moscow

The Daily Telegraph had been on its financial knees when Conrad Black purchased it at the end of 1985. He appointed Max Hastings as editor to restore the paper's standing and recruit a stronger writing team. Max offered me the job of roving foreign correspondent. This promised adventure, independence and a wide writing horizon. I was sure I would enjoy it. I said yes and joined the paper at the end of June 1986.

I went at once to India, Sri Lanka and Pakistan, where there was plenty of reporting to do. While I was in India, gunmen murdered the general who had ordered the army's attack on the Golden Temple, the Sikhs' holiest shrine, at Amritsar two years earlier.

I filled a notebook interviewing Benazir Bhutto at her family's home in Karachi. She sat beneath a large portrait of her late father and spoke with passion, an edge-of-the-seat animation, an intense gaze, determined to restore democracy to Pakistan. At dinner, she said with a smile that her appetite was increasing. 'I use a lot of energy campaigning. The government won't allow me on television. The only way I can communicate is to travel. I feel buoyant.' The next time I saw her she had just been freed after twenty-five days in jail. In India I interviewed Rajiv Gandhi, the prime minister, and went to Nepal to describe the recruiting of young men keen to serve in the Gurkhas. After a spell in Pakistan, I went to Iceland in October to report the first Reagan-Gorbachev summit in Reykjavik. I interviewed a group of Icelanders as we grew as pink as prawns in an outdoor pool. 'We should make Reagan and Gorbachev sit in here,' said one, 'and not let them out until they agree.' The image of the two leaders sitting in a hot pot like a couple of cartoon missionaries made everyone laugh. The summit, as it turned out, was a failure. The leaders could not agree.

I began reporting from Moscow in a seven-week stint during the summer of 1987. I was in a hotel and needed to find my way to the office. Hail a taxi, I was told, and say to the driver 'naprotiv teatr kukol'. It means: opposite the puppet theatre. Everyone knew where the puppets danced. To attract a taxi, I stood on the kerb with a packet of cigarettes in an upraised hand. The red and white Marlboro livery was irresistible, a fly to a trout. Within seconds a taxi or a private car swerved from the herd and was at my side.

From the puppet theatre, I crossed the road to a brown nine-storey apartment building we called Sad Sam, one of more than a dozen buildings in Moscow occupied exclusively by foreign diplomats and journalists. Sad Sam had been built by German prisoners of war. Its nickname derived from its place on a stretch of the Moscow ring road called Sadovo-Samotechnaya. A pair of policemen in a sentry box monitored its only entrance. In my time in Moscow, *The Daily Telegraph*, the BBC, Reuter, the *New York Times* and others had homes and offices in Sad Sam. Apartments in the building were pleasantly spacious with high ceilings, casement windows and parquet floors. We left our cars in the courtyard or the street. Mostly they were Volvos with distinctive yellow number plates. Ours had the number 001, showing it was British, and the letter K for correspondent.

I liked to learn my way around on foot. Sad Sam was half an hour from Red Square. Sometimes, on the way back, I bought bread at Bakery No 675. Following the example of local women, I tested loaves for freshness by squeezing them with the shop's spatula. At the start of the school year in September, I watched pupils arrive in their new uniforms, carrying flowers for their teachers as a band played lively tunes and mothers blinked back their tears.

A covered market nearby sold fruit and vegetables, meat and freshwater crayfish, fairly expensive, for this was a private enterprise market. All the produce was grown in gardens. Many of the customers were foreigners.

On the pavement near our building, Muscovites gathered shoulder to shoulder to study newspapers pinned up in glass-fronted display cabinets. An ice cream shop and a tobacco kiosk always had queues. Lines formed at a liquor shop two hours before it opened at two o'clock. Many in the drinks queue bore an air of defeat. Women complained to the authorities about the shortage of eau-de-cologne, their rare luxury,

111

because alcoholics were buying and drinking it. Outside the liquor shop, drinkers formed quartets to buy and share a bottle of vodka. Once the quartet was complete, its members set off to find a quiet corner in which to empty the bottle. Women wanting sweet Russian bubbly for a wedding or birthday endured the humiliations of queuing, their lives coarsened by the rudeness they encountered.

I walked in streets of charming and characterful houses, primrose, pale green, pink and butterscotch. Some of them were down-at-heel duchesses with sagging sills and flaking stucco. A tall, yellow house had a frieze of bats. As I walked, I heard piano and violin lessons, and saw students at their easels through the art school windows.

In the Hermitage gardens, beneath the rustling trees, I watched the quickfire chess, click clack click, the players banging their fists on the clock, drawing on their cigarettes, watched intently by spectators. Passing the indoor air rifle range, I heard the distinctive spitting of pellets. Bookworms on their benches found contentment. Strollers caressed their ice cream cones. Still others walked toddlers and expensive dogs. Young women linked themselves to soldiers' arms.

I walked south from Sad Sam to the heart of Russia, Red Square. Red and beautiful were the same word in Old Russian. Kremlin, meaning a fortress, is Red Square's citadel, a walled stronghold of passages and secret doors. Through the centuries, all the roads of Russia have met in the square. For a while I watched the people, then threaded my way back through the streets to Sad Sam.

I wrote on my portable typewriter and on a computer contraption rigged to convert text into a telex tape. It made a happy sound on a busy evening, the story chattering its way to London. It would be a perfect disc for a desert island.

Our Russian staff of three was headed by Nellie, the secretary. She looked like Dolly Parton, kept an eye on the news, translated significant pieces in *Pravda*, accompanied me when I needed an interpreter in Moscow. When I wished to travel outside Moscow she telexed the foreign ministry. If the trip was approved, and it usually was, she obtained the tickets. Ira, the housekeeper and cook, was addicted to the regular faith-healing shows on television. She wore plasters on her arms to reduce her weight. Tolya, the driver, drove me to press conferences and interview appointments, and also to the airport and railway station. Like all office drivers he knew where petrol was available. He was a cheerful man with a ready smile. His only word of English was 'lunch'. As I was learning Russian with a tutor and had survived an intensive Berlitz course in London, I talked to him about his family.

As a foreign correspondent I was never part of the crowd boarding a plane. I was either first aboard or last, always escorted to my seat. Once, when I was first, and installed in my seat, I waited a long time. An air hostess, keeping an eye on me, said: 'This plane is very sick.' After a long interval, I was led to another aircraft.

Nellie also made phone calls and wrote letters booking restaurant tables in Moscow. Menus were impressive, but the food actually available was limited. Soviet state restaurants were generally vile, hotel breakfasts often beetroot and cold peas. But in my time in Moscow, private restaurants improved.

The gem in Leningrad was the Literary Café. Alexander Pushkin, founder of modern Russian poetry, walked out of it in 1837 to fight a duel, and subsequently died of his wounds. The title of this chapter is taken from his verse: 'Moscow: those syllables can start/A tumult in the Russian heart.' The Literary Café had an unsoviet atmosphere. No surly bully lurked at the door. Attentive waiters, dressed in white shirts and bottle-green tailcoats, poured Georgian wine. No raucous band played. It was civilized. A pianist accompanied a cellist, perhaps, or three young women in long, black dresses played violins, so soothing. The food was invariably cold meat and smoked fish, the main course grilled meat and potatoes. There was ice cream, too. Always.

★

In November 1987 I wrote from Enniskillen in Northern Ireland about the IRA bombing of a Remembrance Day parade which killed twelve people. One of them was Marie Wilson, a nurse, who, as she lay dying in the rubble, said to her wounded father: 'Daddy, I love you very much.' I went to the funerals. Gordon Wilson's dignity, his rejection of bitterness, was salutary, the crucial phenomenon of the aftermath. In Dublin and throughout the Irish Republic, I saw how much the people were shaken by Enniskillen. When I was back in Belfast, a man looked at me over his beer and said: 'You'll never understand us, we don't understand ourselves.'

I went to Australia in January. The people were marking the 200th anniversary of the arrival in 1788 of the First Fleet and its cargo of convicts, men and women. A celebration was proper and some swagger was in order, but the Australian way was to be self-deprecating and laconic. Some people were embarrassed by the official bicentenary song and would rather have had good old *Waltzing Matilda*. Britain has the seaside, but Australia has the beach, stronghold of the tradition of leisure, essence of the code of 'no probs, no trubs, no worries'. The beach is the social focus, arena of the Oz paseo. The world and his Sheila came to town for Australia's brilliant day. The Prince and Princess of Wales arrived to present Britain's birthday gift, a 200–ton brigantine. I covered their tour from Sydney to Adelaide and Darwin.

I went to write from Hong Kong, Brunei and Singapore, and then reported the unrest in Bangladesh. My luggage was mislaid at Dhaka airport but was found the next day and I went to retrieve it. A uniformed guard took me to a mountain of suitcases. Mine sat at the foot of it. I signed a chit. 'Now,' the guard said, 'you are strictly speaking outside Bangladesh because you are on the airside. But there is a way to get back.' He led me to the luggage conveyor and told me to sit on it with my suitcase. 'Please duck your head,' he said, pressing the conveyor button. Approaching the black rubber fronds of the baggage hatch, I ducked low and emerged on the other side, back in the airport, back in Bangladesh.

I sent reports of the political violence and flew on to cover the troubles in Sri Lanka and killings in Amritsar.

★

After covering the Democratic convention in Atlanta in July 1988, I returned to Moscow, an addictive place for foreign correspondents. Intensity made the heart beat faster. The Soviet Union in the time of Mikhail Gorbachev was a compelling world story. Gorbachev took power as general secretary of the Soviet communist party in March 1985 when he was a bustling fifty-three. The Chernobyl nuclear disaster could not be concealed and ended Moscow's tradition of cover-up. Gorbachev's rule was a diet of amazements. He seemed to have all the ideas when Soviet hardliners had none. To the world's vocabulary he added the words perestroika and glasnost, meaning restructuring and openness. He had a talent for television and frequented the crucial nine o'clock news broadcast on all three channels. Mrs Thatcher, we remember, said she could do business with him. He and Reagan were photographed as ranch buddies wearing Stetsons. Gorbachev cut defence spending and approved the idea of reform in the Baltic countries, Estonia, Latvia and Lithuania. It appeared that the river was running his way. He seemed to be a remarkable man of authority and vision. But in the end, he could not deal with his immense country's diversity and history, nor overcome the enemies of change. He did not know how to secure reform.

Usually I flew to Leningrad, but I liked the overnight train to the Baltic countries. Sometimes people talked in the anonymity of the corridor, drinking tea from the samovar, practising their English. A man told me why he thought Gorbachev would fail. 'Too many bureaucrats with too much to lose. They'll block him, sabotage his plans. They have careers to think of, preserving a way of life that has been good to them. We know how hard it is to change. He can't live long enough. He needs fifty years. A whole outlook must be reformed. It cannot be done in a few years. Gorbachev gives more hope to you westerners than he does to Russians.'

★

In Budapest and Prague I interviewed people about their desire for a new life outside the Soviet orbit. I flew to Canada to write about the changing lives, and the hopes, of Inuit people. For three days, I gathered information at Iqaluit, formerly Frobisher Bay, in Baffin Island. I flew north to the village of Pangnirtung to talk to people there. Conrad Black telephoned me. At that time, we had not met. He invited me to call on him in Toronto. I reached Toronto the following evening, and bearing in mind the advice of the American reporter in Miami, I stayed at the grand King Edward hotel. I saw Conrad the next morning. He was genial, and we talked of the paper and the Canadian elections. He asked where I was staying. 'The King Edward,' I said. 'Good pub,' he smiled approvingly.

A few days later, I flew on an assignment from Cairo to Nairobi, then to Athens to cover the funeral of Christina Onassis. In December, I flew from Moscow to describe the major earthquake in the southern republic of Armenia. It devastated the cities of Spitak, Leninakan and Kirovakan. Tens of thousands of people died in a disaster made worse by bitter December weather and the collapse of badly-built blocks of flats. Soviet authorities were typically slow in mobilizing relief. Coffins were stacked everywhere in rubbled streets and on football pitches. All three cities were grotesque panoramas of fallen buildings. As night fell, a rescue centre in Spitak offered me a stretcher to sleep on. Most of the people in the ruins were dead. A Soviet army officer gave me a lift and we drove forty-five miles to Leninakan. Like Spitak it was piled with coffins. Half a million people were homeless. A man showed me the shattered buildings and said he had buried many of his nephews and nieces.

★

In 1989 I became chief Moscow correspondent. Most Sundays I was up early to write 900 words or so for Monday's *Daily Telegraph*. This was a column, Inside Russia, a journalistic letter about Russian life, humour and humanity. It was different in style and content from the daily headline dramas of Mikhail Gorbachev and the unfolding crises of the Soviet Union. These I would write later in the day, into the evening, with an eye on the time difference between London and Moscow, London three hours ahead.

The guide at Lenin's home was keen to put me right. Interest in the great leader was as strong as ever, he said. He gave me a keen look. 'There has been no falling off in the number of visitors. They have increased. Lenin is the only politician whose authority is indisputable.'

Lenin came to live in his country home, Gorki Leninskye, the year after the Russian revolution of 1917. It is a white and ochre mansion twenty-one miles south-east of Moscow. I walked among the silver birches Lenin loved. His Rolls-Royce was still there, equipped for snow with a half-track drive at the rear and skis at the front. When he was fit he liked to hunt, and his hunting jacket was displayed in the house. His final illness, however, ended his outdoor days and left him virtually speechless, imprisoned in a wheelchair. British workers sent him a smart electric version in 1923, but he never used it.

The house is a tended shrine. The first stop is the telephone room where Lenin shouted down the line. One of his angry notes survives, threatening the phone engineers with execution. The guide reveals some of his wardrobe. At 5ft 5in, Lenin stood an inch taller than Stalin. He died aged fifty-three in January 1924, at 6.50 in the evening. All the clocks in the house are stopped at that time. On his table were the Jack London stories his wife read to him, and a copy of the *Journal of the Communist Party of Great Britain*.

His death provided admirers with a ready-made god, faith and icon. Josef Stalin insisted that Lenin should be embalmed, a sacred souvenir glorifying Soviet rule. In 1941, as German forces invaded Russia, the body was concealed in Siberia. The casting of Lenin statues was an industry. Barely a place in the Soviet Union was without one, often much larger than life, striding forward, declaiming, coat tails flying, a hand pointing to the future. Every city had its Lenin square, every country district a Lenin farm. Forty cities were given the name. In factories and numerous private homes shrines called Lenin corners were created. After the Soviet seizure of the Baltic republics, black statues of Lenin were placed in their capitals, gigantic chess pieces, symbols of possession.

Illuminated like a jewel, clothed in a suit and tie, Lenin's embalmed corpse lies in the red granite ziggurat of his tomb in Red Square. Millions have seen it. I joined the long line across the square to enter the tomb. Newly-married couples went to the head of the queue, as if for a blessing. Stern and tutting guards told men to take their hands out of their pockets and straighten their ties. They ordered women to button their coats. 'Everyone stop talking.' We descended into the dark temple. No one dared whisper. In a pool of light, we saw the glass sarcophagus, Lenin's blue polka dot tie, his familiar head, bald dome, high cheekbones, small beard. No time to stand and stare. Soon we were out, beneath the Kremlin wall.

The tomb has been closed often for chemical maintenance and the fitting of new clothes. Soon after Lenin's death, his brain was removed, preserved in paraffin and sent to the Institute of the Brain in Moscow. The aim was to discover if any link existed between brain structure and genius. In due course, Stalin's brain was also preserved at the institute, and so was Maxim Gorky's. A Russian journalist asked the director what could be said about politicians after study of their brains. 'Nothing, so far,' the director said carefully.

Until the 1980s, the Lenin myth played its part in Soviet ceremonial. I never saw Moscow in the heyday of the great parades of May and September. In Russia, the onset of spring was a time of catkins and hyacinths, the doffing of the fur hats of winter. In Soviet times, spring was signalled by the publication of official slogans in advance of May Day. 'May the deeds of the Great Lenin live for ever!' 'Let universal human values prevail!' 'Toilers in agriculture, raise production!' Red Square was readied for the triumphalist May Day parade with immense carmine portraits of Marx, Engels and Lenin hoisted as validators of the pageant.

By the time I first went to Moscow, imperial decay was all too apparent. I kept as a bookmark my ticket for the 1989 Revolution Day parade. It was signed on the back by Raisa Gorbachev, who came over to chat to reporters. It was the last but one of the great November parades with the tanks and regiments, the generals with their chain mail of medals.

On the following May Day, 1990, the celebration of Soviet unity in Red Square revealed deep frustrations in Soviet society. It was unprecedented. *The Daily Telegraph* front page carried pictures of Gorbachev watching the outburst, demonstrators brandishing their fists. *Kremlin faces May Day defiance*, said the headline, *Gorbachev walks off after crowds jeer at the shrine of Lenin*. I started my report: 'In Red Square yesterday the wheel of history turned dramatically. Here beside the founder's bones, the very shrine and focus of Soviet communism, the crowd condemned the seven decades of communist rule that have beggared their vast land.'

An unofficial parade followed the official one and gave vent to anger and anguish, a bitter catharsis.

★

I first met Russians at Portsmouth when I was a schoolboy aged fifteen. Two warships, *Ordzhonikidze* and *Sverdlovsk*, brought the Soviet leaders, Bulganin and Khrushchev, to Britain for a goodwill visit. Aboard one of these ships, a group of us met smiling Russian sailors who gave us hammer and sickle badges and pungent cigarettes. Meanwhile, the British Secret Service sent Commander Lionel Crabb, a frogman, to measure *Ordzhonikidze*'s propeller. He drowned, leaving the British government with a scandal.

Grigoriy Ordzhonikidze was a Georgian Communist who may have killed himself on Stalin's orders. In thirty years of power, Stalin demanded the killing of millions of people, destroyed the peasantry by execution, deportation and starvation. He signed death lists almost every day. In my time in Moscow a society called Memorial unearthed the killing pits, disinterring thousands of victims, a bullet hole in each skull. Some Russians deplored this cataloguing of Stalin's crimes. To their minds, his tyranny was part of the heroic nation-building. In the town of Gori, Stalin's birthplace in Georgia, I found the shrine to Stalin which once attracted half a million visitors every year. People came to look at Stalin's chair and desk, the photographs of the smiling dictator. They paused by the bronze death-mask lying on a red velvet cushion. For many years, the rooms of the shrine were sealed. A large statue of Stalin stood nearby. After Khrushchev's denunciation of him in 1956, thousands of Stalin statues were removed.

★

At the risk of appearing eccentric, I rigged a mosquito net in my Moscow bedroom. The critters were drawing blood. In Russia, you have to be prepared for anything. I brought cockroach powder as well.

Not so long ago no one would have thought that Gorbachev would call on the name of Jesus to support an argument. But here was Gorbachev telling hardliners of the Russian communist party that if the Soviet economy were not changed only a biblical miracle would save it. 'Only Christ,' he said, 'managed to feed thousands with five loaves.' Christ is mentioned more these days, Marx is mentioned less.

As for Lenin, a reform-minded party member says it is time the corpse were buried. Hardliners would like the topic to remain taboo. Perhaps they dislike the wooden Lenin dolls, the political matryoshkas that artists sell. Maybe they dislike the ambience of places where such things are sold. Arbat Street is such a place, a Moscow bohemia, a street of beards where satirists sing and strum, actors stage pavement revues, long-haired poets declaim and artists work at their easels. The energy and irreverence of the Arbat dismay the people who ache for social discipline. But newspapers, too, show how hard it is to remain in the unchallenged past. *Pravda* lightened its heavy columns, showing beauty contestants with shapely legs. Even *Red Star*, bastion of conservative military thought, carried articles for young soldiers about the once-despised rock and roll. Brezhnev's former tailor recently revealed that after years of wearing grey suits Brezhnev suddenly started wearing blue. Almost overnight the politburo changed to blue, too. I saw the poet Yevgeny Yevtushenko, tall in his striking red suit. On his tie was a painted nude.

As for the beards of Arbat Street, we can be sure that Peter the Great would have reached for his razor. Seizing Russia by the scruff of its neck from 1689 to 1725, he shaved his own beard and cut the whiskers of every nobleman. His beard checkpoints at Moscow's gates had barbers at hand to ensure that no man went hairy into the city. To Peter's mind beards symbolised the hidebound conservatism he detested. Some of his shaved courtiers wept and put their snipped beards under their pillows. To some minds, Gorbachev is no less a barber. Instead of beards they tuck their whiskery ideology beneath the pillow.

In Moscow's summer days the air lies heavy and dusty. A friend and I walk the rutted streets to the old banya. It emits plumes of steam like a leaking saucepan. We buy birch twigs for a rouble apiece and tickets for the bath. This place belongs to old Moscow, a banya of dog-eared grandeur, its mosaics worn and classical columns chipped. In the baronial changing room, heavy pink men sit beached and panting, wrapped in sheets. We enter the steaming gloom where men scrub and flick themselves with birch leaves as horses flick at flies. We submit to the ordeal of the hot room. Old hands wear sopping hats dunked in cold water. Fleeing the furnace, we swim in the roman bath, its columns ivory with age. The banya admits no rank, nakedness is an equalizer, men speak freely in this steamy parliament. In the changing room, a hippo of a man points out the two pedicurists snipping nails and hard skin. 'Only two roubles,' says the hippo, 'makes your feet like new. But go to the old man, he does a better job. The young bloke does it the Soviet way.' The talk turns to politics. 'These people,' says the old man with quiet scorn, 'have been buggering us around from dawn to dusk for seventy years.'

One evening, the gleaming silver birches drew me along a snowy path in Sokolniki Park. I heard distant music and saw a faint glow of light through spindly branches. I had found a secret Moscow, a teddy bears' picnic, an icy arena banked high with snow, lit by a skimpy circlet of lights, yellow, red and blue. I saw a crowd, thickened by fur coats, warmed by hats and scarves, speckled by snowflakes. All middle-aged or beyond, ursine yet gentle, they moved to the rhythm of the tango. When the music faded, the gentlemen bowed to the ladies, as polite as young officers, so that one sensed that romantic hearts beat beneath the thick coats. Waltz, foxtrot, tango, quickstep, they danced the steps learned long ago. The music was Glenn Miller and Victor Sylvester or thereabouts, decidedly forties and fifties. It cost fifty kopeks, Saturdays and Sundays. Women outnumbered men and some of them danced together, gliding across the sanded ice. Some waited, tapping their toes, and did not have to wait long, for every man seemed a gallant. With a 'Please may I...' he drew a new partner into the throng. A woman told me she never noticed the cold, for dancing equalled warmth. 'I come every week,' she said, 'for the music and the romance.' A man of seventy summers gathered her up as Eddie Calvert's trumpet sounded *Cherry Pink and Apple Blossom White*.

Walking from Sad Sam one morning, I saw Yevgeny Yevtushenko again. A dramatic figure as always, six foot three, his blue denim overcoat flapping. He strode across Trubnaya Square and the crowd parted, as if someone had shouted: 'Make way for the poet.' Yevtushenko was directing a film he had written about Stalin's funeral. Even in his coffin, Stalin caused mass death. 'I was here,' Yevtushenko told me, 'in this very square, nineteen years old. A huge crowd came down that hill, hundreds killed, crushed to death against the lorries, trampled under horses' hooves. I understood for the first time that a crowd can be a monster. My film is partly about the end of a monster. It shows that where a dictatorship collapses it can be replaced by another monster, chaos.' The young Yevtushenko was notably anti-Stalin. His readings drew crowds of thousands.

★

Ada was ninety and almost blind. In her small flat in Moscow she reached out to touch my face. She married an Englishman, learned English and lived in London for three years. In the 1930s she returned home and taught English in Moscow. One of her pupils was Nikita Khrushchev, a man full of humour, she said, always skipping classes to do party work. Stalin's secret police arrested Ada in 1938 and interrogated her in the Lubyanka. She was sent to a forced labour camp in the far north and made to cut timber. She saw many prisoners die in the bitter winters. Some removed their outer clothing to quicken their death. Ada was released in 1947, but two years later, in another of Stalin's purges, she was sent to Siberia. She was freed in 1956, her sentences 'annulled in the absence of guilt'. 'In our country,' she said, 'our leaders lied and made liars of many people.'

She retained clear memories of her time in London. A schoolboy on a crowded bus to Hampstead offered her his seat. 'But I am not old,' I said. And he said: 'No, but I am a gentleman and you are a lady.'

★

I flew to Tbilisi, the Georgian capital, to gather words for a column or two. At dinner we had spinach heavy with the garlic Georgians believe is a factor in their famous longevity. Lamb kebabs followed. It was as well we left some room. A scientist invited us to his home and, in the tradition of Georgian hospitality, served caviar, salty cheese, grape and walnut sausage, tea, cheesecake, brandy. As an assurance of sweet dreams, he gave us rose petals in syrup.

There was good red wine, too. It goes with the sunshine Russians envy. Georgians eat, drink, cook and dress better. They insist they smile more. Russians stand in queues, Georgians sit and drink wine.

As for Tbilisi, it has something of Turkey, something of Greece, a dash of the Mediterranean and the Middle East, with courtyards, alleys and wooden balconies. Georgians are notably patriotic and devoted to their culture. They firmly resisted Moscow's attempt to do down the Georgian language in which they live their private life. Politics were complicated. People joke that when five Georgians meet, four will form political parties. Most of them never really wanted to be in the Soviet Union and are keen to get out. How to do it is what they talk about over the wine and roses.

In Leningrad I went to the Fur Palace. Empty seats told the story: the trade was down in the dumps. 'The fur coat,' said a British trader, 'just isn't what it was.' Animal rights campaigners had helped to reduce demand. More importantly the fashion for fur had declined, the fur coat no longer the status symbol it had once been. Pouting starlets no longer draped their shoulders with mink and silver fox. A London buyer said: 'You hear of kids telling their mothers: Don't meet me in your fur coat, Mum, I'd be embarrassed.' One fur not affected by fashion, I noticed, was the exotic sable sold only in Leningrad. Like a rare diamond, a sable coat remains a grand statement of wealth.

Fur is not a luxury in Siberia, as I saw when I travelled in winter to Yakutsk, the coldest city on earth. What you wear is a matter of life and death. Boots of silver-grey reindeer hide are a vital protection. Taking their seats in a theatre, people kept their fur hats on their laps. Thieves trade them for vodka. Hat-snatching is no prank, but a serious crime.

Schools in this part of Siberia close when the temperature reaches minus 51C. Cars have double-glazed windscreens and engines keep running day and night unless parked in a heated garage. Windows in houses are triple-glazed, buildings entered through three sets of doors. The frozen river Lena becomes a dual carriageway complete with traffic lights. Truck drivers carry bricks of beetroot soup to melt for their lunch. When I removed a glove to take a photograph, my hand froze in ten seconds.

I met a couple fresh as bubbles, she in bridal white, he in a new suit, heading from the registry office to their wedding party. 'Please come,' they said, 'it's good luck to have a foreigner.'

'Wonderful,' said Nadia, my guide, 'I hardly ever go to a party.'

A hundred guests thronged restaurant tables piled with a feast of mare's blood sausage, chicken, dumplings, pickles, fizz and vodka. Nadia beamed and said she adored horse meat. As guest of honour, I sat next to the bride's mother, with Nadia on my left. Toasts began at once. The newly-weds were called to stand and kiss to a count of eight. A man sang an old wedding song and the couple kissed to a count of ten.

An accordionist squeezed a few bars of sentiment as prelude to another toast. 'They want you to speak,' Nadia said, 'to bring them luck.' I cobbled some phrases in halting Russian, stood up and spoke.

'Good,' whispered Nadia loyally, 'I understood every word. But anyone can make a speech in Russian. To bring them luck you must speak in English.'

'But no one here speaks a word of English,' I said.

'True,' she said, 'but think, they will remember a toast in English all their lives.'

So I rose to my feet again, made a speech in English and toasted the bride and groom ornately. The room filled with cheering and applause. The band played *In the Mood*.

Nadia said: 'This is what they will remember, the Englishman who blessed their wedding. They will tell their children about it. And their grandchildren.'

In Yakutsk in deep winter, the sun is a congealed egg, appearing for four hours a day. Breath freezes with an eerie crackling, cars usually travel in convoy: a breakdown could lead to a frozen death. Yakutsk is a city on stilts, built on permafrost, the frozen ground that lies beneath half of Russia. A weird spectacle, a cityscape of drunken buildings raised on piles, criss-crossed by heated pipes and ducts carrying water and sewage above the cold surface, the piles as loose as teeth in an old jawbone. In the Institute of Eternal Frost, beneath the ground, the temperature is a constant minus four.

In May 1990, after Latvia declared its independence, a group of us had breakfast in a Latvian hotel. Until the day of freedom, it had been an exclusive club of the ruling party. We had fresh pastries and pancakes, eggs, hot coffee and smiling service. It was a fine morning and we headed south towards Lithuania, bowling along on a good road through a landscape of meadows and birchwoods punctuated by windmills and dairy farms.

Women were out in cottage gardens, men steered horse-drawn ploughs. We stopped to talk to a family. Stanislav was a carpenter and he and his wife Velta were the parents of two girls. As soon as we mentioned independence Velta's tears splashed down her cheeks. 'I was like this last night,' she said, 'so happy I cried and cried.' Stanislav said: 'I cannot forget that the Russians sent my relatives to Siberia. The Russians I like are the ones who demonstrated against Gorbachev.' At a collective farm over the border, a Lithuanian woman said: 'I'm glad the Latvians have joined us in our struggle. You can break one branch over your knee but it is harder to break two. We've had fifty years of hardship. We thought Gorbachev was a god when he started, but now look, he's just another authoritarian.'

Chapter 12

The winter guns

In the autumn of 1988 I went to eastern Europe. For more than forty years the people of Poland, East Germany, Czechoslovakia, Hungary and Bulgaria were part of a Soviet empire and looked to Moscow for direction.

Many Hungarians felt trapped in the Soviet orbit, with all its oppression. The rebellion of 1956 still cast its shadow, the crunch of Russian tanks on cobbles echoing down the years. Pressing their noses to the windows, Hungarians looked wistfully at the western Europe to which, they felt, they belonged. They believed it was their destiny.

Russian visitors to Hungary, however, were gaping at the contrast with their own country. How shabby were the Soviet shops at home, how long their shuffling queues, how hard to get a decent cup of coffee. In Budapest they found well-stocked shops, good clothing, plentiful books, better-dressed people with healthier faces. Hungarians are now free to travel abroad, and Russian visitors joke: 'So there is a future for socialism after all.'

Behind Hungary's state economy is a thriving second economy, one that works. It is a capitalist network in which people run engineering firms and shops, and form a large community of moonlighters. 'When you do your state job, you don't work hard,' I was told. 'You save your energy for your second job, your business.'

I found a similar attitude in Prague. 'People make money, there is plenty of food, you can dream of the weekend,' said a Czech. He sketched an outline of his country. 'We are not cut off. We tune in to western television and radio. I think we are better informed than you because we listen more carefully. Listening to foreign broadcasts is like an act of resistance.' Such freedom and solace exist alongside repression and censored newspapers. In Prague, as in Budapest, the authorities are marooned in the past, and fearful of the new wind blowing. 'People know,' said my Czech, 'that changing the leadership without abandoning the entire system is a waste of time. It would be like changing the dance band on the *Titanic*.'

In the extraordinary year of 1989, the societies of eastern Europe began to break free, as if grasping a rope, hauling themselves from a mire. Communist leaders saw a sudden swing of the compass needle.

In June, Polish voters created the first non-communist government in eastern Europe since 1944. In September, Hungary opened the iron curtain to allow East Germans to pour into the West, committing their country to democracy. In November, East Germany opened the Berlin Wall, a stunning and emotional event. A day after that, Bulgaria ended the thirty-five-year reign of the communist dictator. Two weeks later, Czechoslovakia's people ended the dreary rule of their communist regime. By the end of the year they had elected Vaclav Havel to the presidency. Communism's squandering of human energy was over.

★

Three days before Christmas 1989 the regime of the deranged Romanian dictator Nicolae Ceausescu was collapsing. I hurried to Moscow's Sheremetyevo airport. Nothing was flying to Bucharest, Romania's capital. The country was in turmoil. There was little choice. I flew with a Reuter correspondent to the Black Sea resort of Burgas in Bulgaria. From there we went in a taxi to the Romanian border town of Giurgiu, 150 miles away, on the Danube. We crossed the frontier in darkness. Battles between freedom fighters and Ceausescu's communist troops were ending. A medic insisted on showing us an overcrowded hospital morgue. In one of the wards a communist soldier was chained to a hospital bed. He looked utterly dazed. We rode in a Bulgarian medical convoy to Bucharest, forty miles away. A doctor gave us a lift into the heart of the city. We were stopped by half a dozen boys, aged about fourteen, waving guns, white-faced and maddened. The doctor talked to them, gently calmed them, and they let us through. The doctor dropped us at the Intercon hotel. There was a bullet hole in the front door. The body of a Belgian journalist, recently killed, was in a car outside. Candlelit shrines on the bloodstained pavements marked the places where people were killed by the secret police, the Securitate.

Fighting raged in a nearby square and I walked towards it. A young man appeared and nudged me into a doorway. He told me to wait until the firing subsided. After hours of fighting, he was weary. He said he had learned to handle his gun during his army service. He was excited. 'This is the greatest time of my life,' he said. 'I'm twenty-five and lucky enough to see my country liberated.'

I inched my way and found shelter beside a tree spattered with blood. Unarmed people, crouched and huddled together, urged the soldiers on, cheering and shouting: 'Freedom, freedom, down with the Rat.' The Rat was Ceausescu's nickname. I was seeing not just a battle but an ecstasy.

I noticed a dark-haired girl standing on the edge of the cobbled square, her face tilted up. She was not taking cover. She was absorbing everything, as if filling her memory. People were setting aside fear and caution. Smashed glass and mineral water bottles lay everywhere, in the gutters and over the square. Men emerged from a communist party headquarters, crunching over the glass and carrying stretchers they had filled with fine clothes, perfume and videos and other booty. They had also looted contraceptives, luxuries for the ruling elite, forbidden to the public.

Ceausescu's tyranny, his megalomania during his long reign, reduced millions of Romanians to poverty. His dictatorship banished gambling but he and his illiterate wife Elena had their personal one-armed bandit to play with as they drank from goblets of gold. He had been the president of Romania for twenty-four years, mad creator of vast outsize buildings. Now he and his army of thugs were making a last stand. He resisted the liberal breeze blowing across Europe, kept his people in poverty, used his sinister police to crush opposition. One of his heroes was the fifteenth-century ruler Vlad the Impaler. His greed and gangster morals finally became unendurable to his beggared people. He and his wife enjoyed holidays in their magnificent country houses, hunting trips and sailing on the Black Sea, dinners on golden plates. Romania was not a poor country. Its farmland and oil could have made it rich. But Ceausescu's disordered vision impoverished the people. Bread was rationed in many parts of the country. The dictator sneered and said Romanians ate too much. He was content to live in

In the fast-moving Gorbachev years: the author at his desk in Moscow

The coldest of the cities: Yakutsk, in the Siberian winter

Written in the stars: Ambika in her wedding finery in Delhi

Kidnap in Kashmir, 1994. The author joined David Housego in the search for his sixteen-year-old son, Kim Housego. The kidnappers finally freed Kim and a fellow trekker

Dressed in style: exotic feathers and mud-based make-up for a warrior in Papua
New Guinea

The wildest place I've ever seen – the relentless thunder of the Southern Ocean

Wrapped up warm, holding a course day and night: the author at the helm of *English Rose*

Lifelong adventurers: John and Marie Christine Ridgway, a study in blue at Kerguelen island

Farthest south: landfall at the Rendezvous Rock, Kerguelen

Khyber railway, Pakistan: man versus harsh nature

Andaman Islands, Indian Ocean: high on the hill of Viper Island a gallows building broods

I interviewed and photographed Khan Abdul Ghaffar Khan, famous witness of the old frontier, for half a century the outstanding leader of the Pathans, ninety-seven when he died

Flying from Rawalpindi to Gilgit I had a dramatic view of mighty Nanga Parbat mountain. Returning on the Karakoram highway was another adventure

splendour while 23 million people lived in poverty. He and his wife were always despised.

The Ceausescus fled and did not last long on the run. Soldiers captured them a few miles from Bucharest. On Christmas morning a military tribunal sentenced them to death for genocide and corruption. The tribunal believed no one was safe while 'the imperial couple' lived. Hundreds of soldiers watched the proceedings. At the end, the court called for firing squad volunteers. Every man raised his hand. Three were chosen. Soldiers led the couple to execution.

Elena Ceausescu spoke bitterly to one of them. 'I was like a mother to you,' she said.

'What sort of mother were you,' he retorted, 'who killed our mothers?'

A television camera recorded the gunfire at four in the afternoon. The people had demanded to see the evidence of death. On a television screen in the Intercon hotel we saw the couple slumped at the foot of the execution wall. Ceausescu took Romanian communism with him, into his grave.

No commercial aircraft were flying out of Bucharest. I was offered a lift to Brussels in a Belgian air force freighter. The coffin of the Belgian journalist was put aboard.

★

In the first days of January 1991 a troubling cloud settled over the three Baltic countries, Lithuania, Latvia and Estonia. It could not be ignored. I took the overnight train from Moscow to Vilnius, the Lithuanian capital, and found the city sombre and tense. Gorbachev was raising his authoritarian fist, ordering the Baltic people to surrender independence and submit to Moscow. Lithuania's vice-president construed the choice as 'independence or slavery'. A showdown was in the making.

Next day, Soviet tanks thundered onto the streets. Russian troops seized the publishing house in Vilnius, the place where all the newspapers were printed. Inside they roughed up some of the people. I was in the crowd outside. People were singing folk song choruses and defying the soldiers. On a balcony above us, a young man pointed a hose towards the troops and tried to coax some water from it. As it dribbled harmlessly, a furious colonel seized a Kalashnikov from a soldier and fired at the man. He shot him through the face. I saw the hole in his cheek when he was carried down. I heard later that he had survived. The colonel's bullets peppered the wall. Masonry chippings fell onto our heads. Soldiers fired blank rounds into the crowd. The people linked arms and never flinched. They really were the people: young, middle-aged, elderly. A tank moved close to them and fired a blank shell, a tremendous bang. The people would not give way.

That night, tanks and troops attacked the crowd singing outside the television transmission building. This time the soldiers used live rounds at close range. They fired into the singing people and killed fourteen of them. A blank tank round ripped the night. A young woman spoke calmly of the killings she had just seen. Grasping my arm, she said I must tell people outside what I had witnessed, that the truth should be told before the communists told their lies. As she spoke, the turret of a tank swung slowly and menacingly, the barrel of the gun rising above us. The muzzle of a machine gun inspected our faces.

I went to the hospital and saw doctors at work. Two young men lay lifeless on the floor. Others had been crushed under tanks. Months later, I visited a woman who had been in the crowd that night. A tank track rolled over her and smashed her left leg. She had had surgery and would have some more. She was hopeful. She retained a vivid memory of the soldiers. 'We could all see in their faces that they had come to kill us. I do not feel bitter. Until two years ago I had no hope that freedom would come in my lifetime.'

The day after the shooting, I went to see ten of the fourteen dead. Their coffins were open in the traditional manner, the men dressed in black suits, a woman in a white dress. Relatives kept vigil and a small orchestra played softly. People queued for twelve hours to pay their respects. Next day thousands of people gathered in Vilnius for the funeral, the streets white with snow and black with mourners.

The Russians ordered foreign reporters to leave the capital. We could not stay at hotels. Those of us who remained were offered refuge in private homes. We slept on the floors. Many Lithuanians wished to play a part in getting the news out to the world and drove us around the city.

Their bravery was profoundly moving. They had no weapons. Facing the guns, they linked arms and sang patriotic songs. All they could say was that they loved their country. It was a matter of self-respect. They were not roused by agitators. Their politicians were painfully inexperienced. There were no politics in the half-century after Stalin took their country in the 1940s. Gorbachev was up against simple decency and courage. I had been in Vilnius, some months before, when Gorbachev came to talk to the people. He himself had admitted the breeze that kindled the embers of hope. I saw him wag his finger as people flocked around him. They believed that if they talked to him about their independence there could be a civilized discussion. His answer, though, after his months of browbeating, was tanks in the streets.

A man who had seen the coffins, who had watched the soldiers shooting into defenceless crowds, said: 'What he doesn't understand is that life without freedom isn't worth living. He doesn't understand human nature.'

The people absorbed the blows with dignity. The bravery, witnessed by reporters, could not be blurred by Moscow. Gorbachev's tanks were a final punctuation for perestroika, whatever perestroika was. A note pinned to a tree quipped: For perestroika read tankastroika. A hardline wind was blowing in the Kremlin. Someone painted a poster in Lithuania showing Gorbachev's Nobel peace prize spattered with blood. When Gorbachev came to power, he had encouraged the Baltic republics and they ran with the ball. I saw him in Moscow. He spoke to reporters and blamed Baltic nationalism for the trouble. His attempt at a confident smile revealed unmistakable anxiety.

In March, in Moscow, at a rally in support of Boris Yeltsin, a Russian heard some of us reporters speaking English and said: 'I hope you Westerners are proud of your Gorbachev. You've been his supporters all these years. Well, we don't feel the same way about him. We certainly don't feel like those people who gave him the Nobel prize. He's your Gorbachev, not ours.' Gorbachev resigned in December 1991, after almost seven years in power. The Soviet Union was dissolved, and replaced by the Commonwealth of Independent States.

131

Chapter 13

Epics of distance

Wearing his Aussie bush hat Peter Wright told me his story. There was something of Coleridge's ancient mariner about him. He had a tale, and he would tell it if it was the last thing he did. He had written a book called *Spycatcher*, revealing what he saw as the rotten state of MI5, the British counter-espionage service in which he had worked for twenty years. He was determined to publish. He was relentless and feeling his age, seventy years old with an ailing heart and diabetes. He had retired from MI5 ten years before to pursue his dream of a life raising horses in Tasmania. Heinemann agreed to publish the book in Australia. Mrs Thatcher and Sir Robert Armstrong, her cabinet secretary, acted at once to stop publication. They believed that MI5 agents should retire to the shadows and keep their mouths shut forever.

The drama of Wright's book, heard in the New South Wales supreme court in 1986, was my first reporting stint in Australia. As a court story it had many juicy elements. Consequently, it made headlines every day for five weeks, an absorbing and entertaining spectacle. *Spycatcher* emerged from the espionage scandals of Philby and Blunt, Burgess and Maclean. Peter Wright believed that the MI5 chief, Sir Roger Hollis, had been a Russian mole. Wright's solicitor was Malcolm Turnbull, who at thirty-two was one of Australia's outstanding young lawyers. He relished the case. He had been a Rhodes scholar at Oxford and was able to say to Sir Robert Armstrong: 'Come now, Sir Robert, we are both Oxford men.' The judge was a Rumpolean former intelligence officer who had already observed that the British security services had 'leaked like a sieve for years'.

When Sir Robert had to admit that during his evidence he had been 'economical with the truth', everyone knew what tomorrow's headline would be.

It was summer in Sydney. I swam at the beach early every morning.

At weekends, I sought stories for Monday's paper. I went to the Gabba cricket ground in Brisbane and joined the shouty crowd on the famous Hill to watch Ian Botham in his run-scoring pomp. Then I wrote it up:

'G'day. Here we all are on the Hill at the Gabba in Brizzy. The sun is hot, the Poms are in, our shirts are off and every bloke and Sheila has a chilled tinnie. The principal epithet, roared from hoarse throats, is as unoriginal as it is inevitable: Hit the ball you Pommie bastards. For his part Botham obliges and bows to the Hill – and keeps on obliging for much of the glorious day. Watching Botham lay about him is a pleasure anywhere, but to be a Pom on the Hill on Botham's day is stuff for a grandfather's tale. Here, says a rueful neighbour, handing me a tinnie and wincing as Botham bashes on past his century, lock your laughing gear round this.'

My next weekend assignment during the *Spycatcher* case was different. I went to Alice Springs. The crowd was 6,000 and the star was the Pope.

The great spy case closed a few days before Christmas. I returned to Australia in March. Peter Wright won his case, the book was published and the British government paid the court costs.

★

Captain Cook taught navigation to William Bligh who in turn taught it to Matthew Flinders. In his mid-twenties, Flinders became a protégé of the influential Sir Joseph Banks, a veteran of Captain Cook's first circumnavigation. Flinders was given command of *HMS Investigator*, a 334-ton sloop, and a commission to chart the coast of Australia. No one knew its shape or its size. It was not yet called Australia.

In 1801, Flinders sailed from England to Cape Leeuwin at the south-west corner of Australia. He charted the Spencer Gulf and journeyed up the coast of New South Wales, through the Great Barrier Reef and along the north coast. He noted the harbours that would become Hobart, Brisbane, Perth, Adelaide, and Melbourne. He drew a coastline of 12,000 miles and outlined the shape of a continent to which he gave the name: Australia. It was as large as America, excluding Alaska.

In the 1860s, Australia yearned to connect south to north with a wire and link with the telegraph to London.

John McDouall Stuart set out from Adelaide with horses and an instinct for finding water. I followed his route in a four-wheel drive with plenty of water, from Adelaide into the Flinders Ranges. Trailing a plume of red dust, I reached dog-eared Marree, population fifty, and its gaunt three-storey hotel built in 1885. It was teatime, the bar full of travellers and locals laying the dust with beer. The local historian, Karen Burk, told me of Marree's heyday as a camel transport base. For more than sixty years, into the 1920s, the cameleers drove camel trains across the Australian interior. The forebears of these men came to Australia from Kashmir, Punjab, Egypt, Iran and Afghanistan, but everyone called them Afghans. All they had was their skill and experience with camels. Strings of camels, between thirty and seventy of them, carried mail, medicines, furniture, pianos, everything settlers needed.

In the morning the Marree hotel proprietor made me promise that I would telephone her from William Creek, up the road. If I failed to call her by a certain time she would alert the police. Not long before, on this cindery Martian plain, a woman aged twenty-eight had died of thirst and exhaustion. She broke the first rule, leaving the protection of her bogged vehicle, to seek help. She wandered for eighteen miles before she died.

I kept my promise. I telephoned Marree from William Creek, population sixteen. I drove to the opal-mining town of Coober Pedy where 3,500 people live underground in cool sandstone caves, a warren with subterranean shops, churches and hotels.

I drove to Alice Springs next day, 430 miles, and it was strange, after the desert, to find traffic lights and parking meters. Jose Petrick, a local historian, had worked as a governess on a cattle station and became an outback wife. 'Romantic,' she smiled. *'A Town Like Alice.'*

In 1860, 160 miles north of the waterhole that would later be called Alice Springs, Stuart at last retreated. Almost blind in one eye, limbs aching with scurvy, a wreck in human form, he rode 1,200 miles back to Adelaide.

I flew to Melbourne to follow the epic route of Stuart's rivals,

Robert Burke and William Wills, who started for the north of Australia in August 1860, with a train of wagons, horses and camels. Both were ambitious for glory. But their expedition was torn by quarrels. They risked a midsummer dash for the north coast of Australia. They reached it in 1861, but had not enough food for their return. Starving and exhausted, they reached Cooper's Creek depot to find, in a legendary and tragic scene, that the depot party had quit that very morning. Burke and Wills died of hunger. Their companion, John King, was saved by aborigines.

Stuart started out on a second expedition. He failed, returned to Adelaide and set off again. He reached the Indian Ocean, returning seven months later in July 1862. He nearly died, but made it back to Adelaide. On the day the bones of Burke and Wills were buried in Melbourne, Stuart was the hero of a procession in Adelaide.

In 1870–72, the telegraph was built. An operator tapped the first message on the London–Adelaide line in June 1872. In 1873–74, English cricketers toured Australia and for the first time the scores reached Britain by telegraph. W G Grace was gratified. John McDouall Stuart did not live to see it. He died in London in 1866, all but forgotten.

★

Some of the men I met in Papua New Guinea kept the traditions and inserted bones and pig tusks in their noses. Others, however, preferred a Biro. Ancient rubs against modern everywhere. Tribesmen hunting game with bows and arrows had phone cards to keep in touch with home. Some still fought with spears. Radar speed traps clocked their driving.

Sir Wamp Wan, a distinguished chief in his eighties, showed me the battle scars he had earned as a young warrior: two arrow scars and the purple mark left by a spear in his right thigh. He told me he first met white men in the 1930s. Some thought at first that these creatures might be ancestral spirits. The first wheel Sir Wamp ever saw was on the aircraft that brought them to his homeland in the western highlands. Soon he was the first of his tribe to own a bicycle, later the first to have a car. My flight to the highlands was delayed, not by a tribal skirmish but by a glitch in the Air Niugini computer. Sir Wamp was a man rich in honour, wives, children, pigs and rare seashells. His services to his country had earned him a knighthood. He thought that Australia's gift of independence in 1975 was too early. Too many young men were troublemakers. As he put it, crime and unemployment had made things go buggerup.

Pidgin is the lingua franca among Papua New Guinea's 700 languages. Men sat at Sir Wamp's feet and translated from pidgin. Those who use English do so with an Australian twang and say 'G'day,' and 'No worries.' Each copy of *Wantok,* the weekly pidgin newspaper, was passed on to twenty other readers and ended up being wall decoration or cigarettes.

Riggo Nangan, the town clerk of Mount Hagen, a dedicated and ever-smiling man of twenty-eight, told me he was saving to get married. His girlfriend's father had named a bride price of £1,950. Riggo said that once he had saved half the bride price, he would ask the bank to lend him the rest.

'I'm lucky,' he said, 'that her father doesn't want pigs or cassowary birds. A pig costs £300. Father-in law is an elder in the Baptist church and I'm a Baptist, too. You should see our churches on Sunday. Always full, but sometimes you get fights between congregations, like tribal fights.'

Fighting is a seemingly ineradicable tradition. A British businessman who had been in the country for ten years said it was a safer place than many others. 'It's learning to walk, a country in transition, in some ways it's 1066 with mod cons. I wouldn't live anywhere else.'

Papua New Guinea is twice the size of Britain. From an aircraft, I looked at the thick forest that covers three-quarters of the country. There was still a sense of land unexplored. On air navigation maps, white spaces are marked Limits of Reliable Relief Information.

I had a lift in a truck to see a singsing, a village ceremony where everyone was painted and wearing costumes of bird of paradise feathers and beads and seashells. Their bodies glistened with tree oil.

I stayed at the copper mine town of Tabubil, population 6,000, near the Ok Tedi river in the western mountains. It had a luxury hotel and a rugby ground. All the food and supplies, all the steak and eggs, the beer and garlic prawns and house wine, are transported by ships up the mighty Fly river, then loaded into truck convoys for the last eighty miles through the forest.

I met computer operators at a gold mine whose fathers encountered the first white men entering the remote and rainy highlands as late as 1963. There's a collision between the customs of traditional societies and western ideas of democracy and business. The parliament is magnificent, complete with soothing shades of House of Commons green. In Port Moresby, the capital, I went to see the newspapers go to press. They were running an exposé of political corruption. The prime minister told me that 'the free press and independent judiciary are among our strong points'. As for being prime minister, 'it's like a rollercoaster, exciting. Sometimes too exciting'.

Capinny Cook, the Maori called him. In his three Pacific voyages he came to Ship Cove five times between 1770 and 1777, staying 100 days in all. As an admirer of James Cook I looked forward to exploring his famous anchorage at the northern end of the South Island of New Zealand. 'A very snug cove,' he called it, a seaman's choice.

Here Cook's ninety men careened their ship *Endeavour* on the beach and scraped the hull clean of barnacles and weed. They made a forge to repair ironwork, cut timber for water casks and foraged for wild celery and other anti-scorbutic greens. Cook climbed to the top of Motuara Island near the cove and named the sound after Queen Charlotte.

Early in 1770 he headed into the Tasman Sea and steered for Australia. As New Zealand slipped from his view, he looked back at the cape and named it Farewell.

Chapter 14

Africa days

CATALINA BABY, 1989

Swooping swan-like to the Nile, the Catalina alighted gracefully in a burst of spray. Watching from the riverbank, Pierre Jaunet rejoiced in this elegant curtsy of a splashdown, the long-awaited amerrissage. His beautiful white flying boat at last in Cairo, the adventure could begin. I felt certain he would kiss her on the nose. He was, after all, French.

The pilots, Jim and Ollie, had flown her halfway across the world, from Vancouver to Newfoundland, to the Azores, Lisbon, Montpellier and on to the Nile. Pierre, 'un chef d'expedition qui connait l'Afrique comme sa poche', dreamed of romantic air safaris, from Cairo to the Victoria Falls, following the old Imperial Airways routes. His adventurous clients would arrive on lakes and rivers and spend their starry evenings in historic hotels and desert camps.

We half-dozen correspondents were cast as trailblazing pioneers. The Catalina was built for long-distance maritime warfare in 1944 and, in 1989, was older than most of us.

Pierre signed the last of the paperwork and we boarded towards sunset. Jim, the captain, was a burly Alaskan of few words. His previous job was water-bombing forest fires in America, all in a day's work. Now, on the Nile, he started the twin engines. The Catalina roared along the river and lifted her nose, reaching for the sky. As she rose in the last of the light the pyramids flashed a farewell gleam of gold.

We touched down on the airstrip at Luxor an hour later. As we did so, the spinning nose-wheel sprang back into its housing and the keel struck the runway in a shower of sparks. Jim pulled up in an instant and we went round again. This time the nose-wheel was safely locked down.

Next day we explored Luxor's wonders, then set off for Aswan and the Old Cataract hotel, sailing the air with a felucca's grace. Our splashdown on the Nile beside the colossi of Abu Simbel was a thrilling moment for Pierre and his wife. It was exciting for us, too. They inflated the orange dinghy and took us ashore to picnic on claret and cheese from Poitiers, Pierre's home, of course.

He gazed at his Catalina like a lover. 'She's beautiful,' he said softly.

In Khartoum we inspected relics of Gordon, of Kitchener and the battle of Omdurman. We visited the junction of the White Nile and the Blue where the Imperial flying boats used to take to the water. Our flight the following day, from Khartoum to northern Kenya, took almost eight hours. Behind the wings, where once were machine-gun turrets, we sat comfortably in the bulbous blister windows and gazed at the slowly unfolding landscape of tawny deserts and mountains. Pierre served a small Poitiers picnic. In the late afternoon light we cut a wake on the jade waters of Lake Turkana. As we anchored we were warned of the presence of crocodiles. We boated most carefully to a lodge on the shore and saw nothing of lurkers.

At take-off next day, Jim played horse whisperer to his Catalina. 'C'mon, baby,' he murmured, racing the old girl across the lake. 'C'mon, baby.' His big hands hauled us from the water's grip and he turned left at a volcano and steered for Nairobi. When we landed Ollie pulled out a bung to release Turkana water from the bilge.

From Nairobi we flew to Arusha in Tanzania and drove to the spectacular volcanic amphitheatre of Ngorongoro, brilliant and busy with wildlife. Jim reported that one of the Catalina's engines needed replacing. Pierre had hoped to make it to Victoria Falls; but we were happy with the adventure we'd had in his elegant swan. The flying boat safari became a success.

NOT FORGETTING THE INVITATION CARDS, 1993
The coronation of the king would be on a sacred hill near Kampala. The evening before the ceremony I walked the steep path and slept on warm red earth in the press tent.

In 1966 Uganda's brutal ruler overthrew King Freddie, the kabaka, or king, of Buganda, the largest kingdom of old Uganda. Freddie died three years later. His son, Ronnie, grew up in London. When he was a schoolboy Ugandan exiles in Chelsea stood him on a chair and hailed him as kabaka. Ronnie studied in London and, for a brief time, was a double-glazing salesman.

Milton Obote and Idi Amin laid waste to Uganda for twenty years, but under a new president, Yoweri Museveni, the country recovered. Museveni ran political risks in restoring the thousand-year Buganda monarchy, but in 1993 Ronnie returned to take up the crown.

King Ronnie himself could not afford the ceremonial costs. A businessman, however, spoke soothingly to him. 'Sir,' he said, 'history will say there was a man who stood behind the people and when they wanted a coronation for their king he told them, yes, you shall have it. It is my privilege to have paid for the royal crown, the ring, the robes, the coronation throne. Not forgetting the invitation cards. My name will be written in history and I can die content.'

I asked the businessman about the expense, but he gently chided me. 'No gentleman,' he said, 'makes a gift to a king and then reveals the cost. Money was no object. The crown is of gold plate, made by a top goldsmith in Bombay. Similarly the ring. The coronation robe is of the finest material, and the throne was assembled by Egyptian craftsmen and delivered by British Airways.'

On the great day King Ronnie was enthroned in brilliant pageantry. Adorned with a robe and a leopard skin he rode on the bowed shoulders of a sturdy tribesman who had supporters at each elbow to steady him. Thousands of shouting men, thousands of ululating women, hailed him. In this fashion an amiable man of thirty-eight repaired the link with a thousand years of history. His people saluted him as King Ronnie. They also called him Stronglegs.

A DAY IN HHOHHO, 1992

From Mbabane, the capital of Swaziland, I drove north through brown and red hills to Hhohho. It was a day of ceremony. King Mswati III was there. He was also known as The Inexplicable, the Sire of the Herd and The Lion. In the telephone directory, however, he was listed modestly and alphabetically as His Majesty, immediately after Hisham's estate agency. Hhohho's crowd was in Sunday best, traditional robes and monkey-skin kilts, girls dancing in beaded skirts, young men stomping the ground to the thump of drums, a choir singing. Two queens sat beautifully, as elegant as ibises. The king wore a red robe and scarlet feathers. In keeping with tradition, he marries frequently to keep the country united. He is very rich and has thirteen palaces. His wives are also big spenders.

Swaziland became independent in 1968. Mswati was fourteen when he went to Sherborne school in Dorset. Crowned king in 1986, he had to set a course between tradition and political modernity: to be, or not to be. The matter has not been resolved. The people, meanwhile, embrace football and follow such teams as Dribbling Wizards, Two Sticks Comrades, Hungry Lions, Black Terrors, Real Toasters, Potato XI, Burning Spear, Never Die and Typing Chiefs.

POISON ARROW, 1994

The telephone rang at home. I was told to go to Africa. Thugs had attacked tourists in a remote district of Tanzania and had killed a young Canadian with a poison arrow. I flew to Nairobi and crossed into Tanzania. At Arusha I hired a Land Rover and a driver and left next morning for the Serengeti plains. We stayed overnight at a lodge and drove next day on the rough road to Issenye. I was told about the attack. A lorry with fifteen tourists and a crew of three, making a five-month tour from West Africa to Nairobi, set up camp in the bush near Issenye mission school. They cooked supper and turned in. At midnight, a gang attacked their tents with machetes and arrows. The tourists ran for shelter in the truck. An arrow struck the leg of thirty-year-old Robert Collier, a lumberjack. He was taken to the mission school. Maureen Jones, the mission nurse, from Yorkshire, told me she set up an intravenous drip and gave heart massage. 'But he was gone,' she said. 'A police officer took one glance. Poison arrow.'

Robert was cremated at Arusha. No tourists had ever been attacked before in this district, a policeman said, but feuds over cattle stealing were sometimes settled with poison arrows. Camping beneath the stars, said a tour manager, was 'one of the reasons people go on safari, the magic of Africa'.

141

A WHITE DOVE, 1994

News from Africa has often been of cruelty and chaos. The upcoming South African election, with its gathered hopes and fears, was an epic, a story for the world. In seven weeks of travel and writing, I was moved by much of what I saw. I listened hard. It had been a time of great violence. Between the 1980s and 1994, more than 15,000 people died in clashes in Natal and Johannesburg.

We were seeing an end and a beginning. The 10,000 Zulus I met in Natal marched along a broad highway, defying the government's emergency laws against the carrying of weapons. They chanted and thwacked their staves, knobkerries and spears on cowhide shields. Wisely, the police took no action. 'You see,' said a man, tapping a knobkerrie, 'this is part of my culture. Without it I would feel uncomfortable, not a full Zulu.' The men lunged their staves into the air and chanted bravely, and that was that. This was South Africa's first election by universal suffrage. The mercurial Zulu chief Mangosuthu Buthelezi threatened to boycott the election. He ran out of followers and called off the boycott.

On polling day I went to Rorke's Drift in Zulu country and saw how passionately people wanted to build South Africa's bridge into the future. Many walked dozens of miles to vote and queued from dawn to dusk. At Pomeroy there were long waiting lines. Two thousand people lined up to be photographed and issued with temporary voter cards. 'It's total disarray,' the election agent told me. 'Many of these women have been waiting three or four days, sleeping rough, getting hungry and thirsty. No one makes them do it. They just want to vote. Makes you think, doesn't it?'

I saw Nelson Mandela meeting crowds at sports stadiums. In his victory was the ending of apartheid, the dream come true. The photograph of his taking part in a celebratory dance, slim and elegant in his grey suit, waistcoat and striped green and black tie, was on the world's front pages. 'We are free at last,' he said. This was the landfall to which the African majority directed their aspiration, even when it seemed unreachable. We had witnessed a revolution. There were bound to be misgivings and fears. But that time belonged to hope. Everywhere people ran through the streets leaping and skipping. My colleague Alec

Russell and I went to the parliament in Cape Town to see Mandela elected the first black president of South Africa. This was the crowning of his journey. He was seventy-five years old. For many years, his view of Table Mountain had been very different. As Prisoner 466/64 he had spent eighteen years of his twenty-seven-year sentence in Robben Island. He remained a tall, straight, dignified man, wise, gentle, utterly determined. Afrikaners had found that adherence to an authoritarian regime relegated dignity. From the balcony of Cape Town city hall President Mandela looked out over a sea of cheering people. He released a white dove. He made a hero's speech. The dream had come true.

The following day we went to Pretoria to see him inaugurated at the Union Building, a former bastion of white power. South Africa's return to the international fold was also celebrated. 'Humanity,' the president said, 'has taken us back into its bosom.' On this day, too, with every word and gesture, Nelson Mandela placed his imprimatur of modesty and dignity.

THE SILENCE OF THE PYRAMIDS, 1998
Terrorists killed fifty-eight tourists at Luxor, beside the Nile. Thousands of people cancelled their holiday trips. *The Times* sent me to Egypt to talk to the small number of British people who were not deterred. Mrs Bennett was there, cruising the Nile and having the tombs almost to herself. She had long dreamed of a Nile holiday. 'We all face risks in everyday life,' she said. 'I'm having a wonderful time.' Three Welsh lawyers had chosen a reunion trip in Egypt and were determined to go. I saw plenty of armed policemen on duty. On a Nile river steamer with room for a hundred passengers there were just twenty-eight of us. My cabin steward left me a note. 'Please come back soon. Best wishes, Aladdin.'

THE CLOSEST ENCOUNTER, 1999
A legendary figure in Africa, Soren Lindstrom was a gifted safari guide, a big, blue-eyed, fair-haired Dane. He learned to be a guide and hunter in Kenya, Tanzania and Sudan, where some of the clients

were the Hemingway and Hollywood sort. He moved to Botswana in the 1970s. 'A fresh start in paradise,' he said. In 1999 I flew from the frontier town of Maun. He was waiting in the Okavango Delta. I had been told about his scars, but it was some time before he related the story himself.

Within minutes of our setting off in his Land Cruiser he whispered: 'We're in luck.' Six bull elephants nearby were chomping contentedly. Soren softly described their feeding and social habits. He took pride in being a naturalist and an enthusiastic teacher. We soon encountered antelope, giraffe, zebra, baboons and warthog, and the remains of an impala which, fleeing wild dogs, dashed into a pool and the jaws of a crocodile. He showed me fish eagles, bee-eaters, storks and lilac-breasted rollers.

Late in the afternoon we watched a hundred elephants marching over the plain, rustling like taffeta. 'This is something wonderful,' Soren said. 'You'll never forget it.' At sunset a group of us had drinks by a fire followed by supper in a tent. We turned in. In the small hours I awoke with my neck prickling, hearing lions calling each other in a low and belchy rumble.

A couple of days later Soren told me of his close encounters with animals. Most dangerously, an injured lion charged from the undergrowth, breaking and almost severing his right arm.

'I didn't have a chance. Luck saved me. One of my trackers had fled into the undergrowth. He moved and alerted the lion. It went after him but he escaped. With the lion diverted, I dragged myself out, reached the car fifty yards away, blood pouring from a severed artery. I had three clients in the car. I got the man to radio for help while the two women pressed their thumbs on the artery. There wasn't much time. A pilot landed a doctor who clamped the artery, fitted a drip and gave me morphine. Doctors in Maun stabilized me and put me on a plane to Jo'burg. A helicopter took me to hospital. It was a close thing, gangrene and skin grafts. The surgeons saved the arm. You can see that the elbow is locked solid. I never tire of bush life, showing people birds, animals and plants. When you've been in the jaws of a lion, every day seems especially beautiful.'

WALK ON THE WILD SIDE, 2000

Walking in the Serengeti bush is not for everyone. There's a certain tingle to it. We walk in single file, silent in the dawn. No guns are permitted. Our safety depends on three Masai trackers. Two carry spears, the third a bow and a quiver of arrows. Using such simple weapons, each warrior has killed a lion to prove his courage. Each wears a tunic, sandals and a cloak and carries a short sword, making me think of Roman soldiers. The leading warrior stops suddenly, pointing to distant acacias. Through binoculars we see a king-size lion watching us. He has a dark mane. His full belly almost touches the ground. He exits slowly. We watch in breathless silence. Mark Houldsworth, our guide, says quietly: 'We'll give him plenty of room.'

A tall Scot aged thirty-nine, Mark is a pioneer of walking safaris. 'At eighteen, I rode my motorbike for a year around Kenya and Tanzania, helping in bars and safari camps, meeting a lot of go-for-it people. I was hooked. I wanted a life in Africa, not in a suit.'

The thrill of a walking safari can't be felt in a vehicle, he says. 'Walking means you keep your distance. You smell and feel the land, aware of every detail. You feel more alive. If you grow hot and tired, that embroils you even more in the landscape.' Like the Masai Mark reads the bush, aware of wind direction, the habits and capabilities of animals. We silently detour around buffalo and elephants with calves.

We drive to see hippo and crocodile, drifting herds of thousands of migrating wildebeest, strobing zebras and a totter of giraffes. On my last morning, Mark suggests an early trek before I head for the airstrip: the special tingle. In dawn's lovely light it's a bonus.

Chapter 15

A gnarly dude

John Ridgway is on the phone. 'Like to sail the Atlantic?' he says. 'Of course,' I say. 'Good,' he says, 'you can't postpone adventure. Adventure is proof of being alive.' He has had plenty of it in his time. He served in the Parachute Regiment and the SAS. As a soldier he got to know the Brecon Beacons the hard way. In 1966 he and Chay Blyth rowed across the Atlantic in a twenty-foot wooden dory, an open boat without shelter. They battled from Cape Cod to Ireland in ninety-three days. John still has the boat, *English Rose III*, in a shed. Some of the oars are still on board, along with battered clothing and goggles and a little store for the curries. The boat has the look of a relic from a Victorian expedition. Every plank spoke of fortitude, the men's hands made claws by the rowing. During the epic struggle, John planned the adventure school he and his wife Marie Christine would build at Ardmore in the far north-west of Scotland, a few miles south of Cape Wrath. Their daughter Rebecca inherited the love of adventure and paddled a kayak around Cape Horn. John skippered his yacht *English Rose VI* twice around the world, the second time non-stop. He and Marie Christine also explored the Peruvian highlands. They adopted another daughter, Elizabeth.

I first met the family at Ardmore in 1993. They were stowing stores for an eighteen-month voyage to the Caribbean, Panama, Galapagos, Tahiti, Chile, Cape Horn, Antarctica and Tristan da Cunha.

'The family is the reason for the trip,' John said. 'It's time I did something more leisurely. I've been in a rush in my first fifty-five years. But all you have is time, so keep wriggling about.'

John, Marie Christine and Rebecca agreed to write running commentaries on their adventure in *The Daily Telegraph*. I went to see them off and wrote an introductory feature for the paper. Towards the end of their voyage, I flew to the Azores to join them in the ten-day sail back to Scotland.

In 2000 John had a new mast fitted at Burnham-on-Crouch and I took part in the voyage back to Ardmore by way of Land's End, Fastnet and western Ireland.

Now for the Atlantic. Most sailors take the easier southern trade wind route. Typically, John opts for the tougher northern route against the prevailing wind and current. Before we sail I spend a few days aboard learning the ropes, filling a notebook with details of power switches, radio, radar, autopilot, engine care, pumps and the galley stove, and noting where the sextant and the emergency tiller are stowed. With Bob Duncan from Zimbabwe and Teije de Jong from Holland we are a crew of four. Before we leave we are joined for dinner by Denise Evans, an intrepid sailor of seventy-three, pausing at Ardmore on a voyage from the Menai Strait to Spitzbergen.

We sail on a dazzling morning, 22 June 2001, rounding the northern end of the Isle of Lewis as the mainland mountains fade. Steering for north America, we pay our respects to solitary Rockall. The sea changes from green to deep dark blue. John Ridgway wants to see how his new gear performs; but mostly we sail for adventure, crossing a part of the Atlantic that in these modern times rarely sees a sail. For company we have seabirds and dolphins; here and there, whales are blowing. We slip into a rhythm of sailing and sleeping, musing and reading. As an amateur baker TJ gives us our daily bread.

On fine and quiet nights the bow is a ploughshare turning the sea and I revel in my watch from midnight to two o'clock. There is no true darkness in these high latitudes. Sunset lingers like the embers of a cottage fire. For the time being I have the ocean to myself. Bob and TJ sleep in the fo'c'sle. The skipper dreams in his doghouse bunk. *English Rose* dips and rustles on a moonlit path.

Soon enough, though, the seas rise up and queue to throw us a punch. We stagger in the saloon, seeking handholds. A great wave gives us a blow and John seems to be horizontal in mid-air, hurting his ribs as he lands. 'This is the place for bad weather,' he says.

We are all on deck one morning when the wind blows John's favourite red hat into the ocean. At once he says: 'We'll make this a man overboard drill and see how long it takes.' We turn the yacht and I point steadily at the hat. I lose sight of it but from higher waves I see it again. It takes a while to manoeuvre and fish it out with a pole. John says: 'Eighteen minutes. We can do better.' But he's pleased to have his hat back.

Every day, during my six-to-ten morning stint, he opens a single eye and says: 'How're you doing, old top?' and I say I am in good order and all's well. From his bunk he can see the compass and our position. At the end of my morning watch I wash and shave. John dislikes stubble. If you won't look after yourself, he says, you won't look after the boat. In rough weather, you might draw blood, but you feel better.

On his birthday, John hands out chocolates from his stash, rum babas all round. We enter the immensity of the Grand Banks of Newfoundland, wrapped warmly against the chill, the headwinds, icy spray and dense fogs. Aware that during a night in May *Titanic* struck an iceberg south of our track, we keep an eye on the radar. For 400 years, before they were fished out, the Grand Banks were the richest of fishing grounds. Thousands of men perished here in their hunt for cod.

We are awed spectators of electrical storms, the sky ripped by lightning. With more than passing interest we read Sebastian Junger's book *The Perfect Storm*, the grim story of a fishing boat overwhelmed in these waters. Free of fog at last, we pass St John's, Newfoundland, and round Cape Race. We start down the Nova Scotia coast in sunshine, then slip into more fog. We pass Cape Sable and put the clock back an hour. After thick fog in the morning, we enjoy a brilliant day.

We steer for Cape Cod where *Mayflower* and her puritan cargo arrived in 1620 to wash their hands of England forever. More than 2,000 nautical miles from Cape Wrath, we see the American coast as night falls. There is no sense in attempting a passage through Nantucket Sound in darkness. We sail gently back and forth through the night, looking at the shore lights. We find a river berth in the sunny morning after a passage of twenty-three days.

Bob and TJ stay for a while and go on their way. John is joined by Marie Christine and their daughter Elizabeth who will sail back with us. I meet Penny in Boston. Richard Morris–Adams, ex–Royal Marine, an old friend of John, joins us, too. John is keen to see Cape Cod and we drive out to Nauset beach and walk to a distinctive brown rock. On it is a plaque commemorating 'the adventure of John Ridgway and his fellow soldier Chay Blyth who set out from this very rock in their twenty-foot wooden dory and rowed it across the Atlantic and landed on the Irish coast'.

John kisses the rock. He recalls the scene of departure. 'A big crowd swarming around us, people wanting to be the last to shake our hands. I felt like a man on the scaffold.' Later in the day people gather to meet John and listen to his story. 'Well,' says one of the audience to me when the tale is told, 'that guy is a real gnarly dude.' This I translate from the American as admiration for a rugged bloke.

We cross Nantucket Sound, 25 July, and head into the Atlantic. Everyone is sick, a gale blows and we are hammered with heavy rain for four more days, the seas breaking into white peaks on dark water. A week after leaving Nantucket, just beginning to feel better, we submit to another gale. On day ten, there is no breeze at all and the sun shines. A beef curry is just the thing. Later we get a southerly gale and sail under a reefed foresail. A storm petrel flies into the cockpit and cannot get out. I grasp it gently and launch it into the air. On day thirteen Penny is called to the cockpit and we serenade her in sunshine on her birthday. On the twenty-fourth day, we sail through the sunny Minch and next day pick up the mooring at Ardmore. We have dinner with champagne. Two days later we are back in Wales and I start work on a television programme, swaying a little, a reminder of our rolling progress across the Atlantic.

Chapter 16

A wedding, rhinos, lions and doubt control

Jitendra was a year old when he was marked out as a husband for the newly-born Ambika. They were introduced in their teens at Corbett Park, the game reserve in the Himalaya foothills and, just as their families had hoped, they liked each other. They shared an interest in wildlife and photography and were engaged when Jitendra was eighteen and Ambika seventeen.

Little of significance is performed in India unless the astrologers are consulted. Matrimony is certainly too important to be left to chance. The marriage of Ambika and Jitendra was first planned for November, but Jitendra's grandfather was troubled by the winter date. The astrologers returned to the charts and found an auspicious opening on a spring day at 3.20 am.

Jitendra's grandfather was the 86-year-old Maharaja of Alwar in Rajasthan. The British deposed his great-grandfather, Sir Jai Singh, in 1933. Some of the stories about him sound apocryphal. Jitendra told me a true one. Sir Jai Singh went to London and visited a Rolls-Royce showroom. He said he wished to buy a car. The English salesman was irritatingly snooty and wondered if an Indian could afford a Rolls. Sir Jai at once ordered seven and had them shipped to India. It became well known that he used them on the streets of Alwar as dustcarts. Among other cars, Sir Jai owned a custom-built Lanchester. On his death in 1937, it became his hearse. He was installed in the back seat, his sunglasses on his face, and driven though Alwar while his subjects wept.

Jitendra told me he was not opposed to traditional arranged marriages providing the couple had the chance to get to know each other. 'My grandfather,' he said, 'did not see his bride until after the wedding ceremony, and I did not want that.'

Ambika's father Brijendra orchestrated the wedding. On the maidan in front of his house in Delhi, 200 agile scaffolders raised a great cotton tent, the colour of a sunflower, appropriately gorgeous for a wedding. Another tent, bright yellow, rose over the marriage pavilion on the front lawn of Ambika's home. Garland makers, hand-painters and singers were recruited. Long lines of marigolds hung over the garden. Good luck coconuts were placed each side of the front door. Servants bustled in saffron turbans. The house and pavilions filled with aunts, uncles, cousins and laughter. There was a smell of coffee, spice, incense and perfume, and the spectacular swirl of saris, red, orange, gold and peach.

The ceremony began with the sound of a conch. A priest sang a haunting song. Ambika wore a saffron sari edged with scarlet. Her mother and grandmother coated her arms with a bright paste of turmeric and sandalwood. Inside the garden pavilion the light was soft and golden. Priests chanted mantras, invoking and propitiating the gods, beginning the ceremonial parting of the bride from her family.

Upstairs a grey-haired man tied magenta turbans around the heads of male guests. We went in white cars to see Jitendra, taking him trays of fruit and sweetmeats. We entered a garden pavilion where musicians played. Jitendra sat on a red carpet, attended by four bearers in yellow turbans and white tunics. Two of them agitated the air with whisks. Jitendra wore gold slippers, a long coat of pale green brocade, a pearl collar and a red and green turban with a jewel. He carried a curved sword. Those approaching him made a circle with their fingers around his head to ward off the evil eye. In accepting the gifts he became irrevocably engaged to Ambika. We joined him for a memorable lunch.

At Brijendra's house that evening we attended a reception and dinner, all of us gathered on the lawn beneath glowing lights. Men sipped Scotch. Women danced to the rhythm of drums, others sat on cushions to talk.

Leading a dazzling gathering of clans, Brijendra wore a princely coat of white brocade. A swagger of maharajas, a score or more, were a pageant in their own right. They stood tall and straight-backed, men with crisp military moustaches and regimental ties, dark jackets and jodhpurs. Jitendra arrived to be ceremonially greeted as he entered the house. After another feast, there was time for a little sleep before the marriage service began in the early hours.

For this Jitendra wore a golden coat and a jewelled turban. He carried a sword. Ambika wore the gift of Jitendra's family, a magenta sari, sixty years old, hung with beads, silver and jewels. Her face was concealed.

An altar was set with grapes and pomegranates. Bells tinkled and a conch sounded. Four men helped Jitendra with his golden coat, his turban, jewellery and sword. Priests lit a fire. Joined together by a cloth, the couple made seven circuits of the fire and fed the flames with puffed rice so that smoke billowed into the air. At last the ceremony ended with drumbeats and hugs.

Soon there was a breakfast of coffee and spicy potato cakes. The married couple said their farewells to the family. Cheeks gleamed with happy tears. Brijendra's wedding present to Jitendra was a white car. The couple climbed into it. A motorcade, preceded by a police Jeep, was filled with wedding presents and set off for Alwar 100 miles away. We travelled in the convoy.

As we crossed into Alwar, local men fired a shotgun feu de joie. The cars swept into the Phool Bagh palace, Ambika's new home. In keeping with custom, she had not seen it before. The staff and local people gathered, smiling and delighted. On the palace walls hung portraits of the rulers of Alwar. Jitendra said he looked forward to playing his part.

'To have a young couple at the palace,' said one of the welcoming party, 'is a beginning for all of us.'

★

Beep-beep went the car as we hurried through the Assamese dawn. I had been looking forward to this trip for years. In my time as a correspondent in India the north-eastern state of Assam was off limits, beautiful country made sad and dangerous by a violent insurgency. In gun battles and murders thousands were killed.

More than thirty years later Assam was safe enough for visitors. The doors were opening. We arrived at a ferry point on the great

Brahmaputra river. The truck ahead of us sported a road safety sign saying: Hurry Hurry Spoils the Curry. Dilip, my driver, zoomed past anyway. He curved around the cattle and goats on the road and headed down a rough track to the river. A team of ferry hands manhandled planks to fashion a ramp and, with shouting and waving, urged Dilip aboard. He perched athwart the ferry with the front and rear of the Jeep overhanging the hull. The ferrymen chocked the wheels with rocks and soon we were off, absorbed into the pearly grey watercolour of the Brahmaputra.

No charts or instruments guided the steersman's serpentine course. He seemed to feel his way through the shifting shoals and shallows. I sat entranced. Waterbirds flocked on the shores and sandbanks. I watched the traffic of ferries crowded with passengers, motorbikes and cattle.

We took almost three hours to reach Majuli island, an estate of rice fields and monasteries dating from the sixteenth century. The myth of the goddess Sati, who was chopped into many pieces, says that this is where her left breast fell to earth, creating life in the island. More than half of Majuli's 2,200 monks are bachelors. The rest have families.

The iconic beast of Assam is the Great White rhinoceros. Its distinctive single horn persuaded early explorers that they had found the unicorn of myth. The African rhino has two horns. Around 2,400 rhinos live in Nepal, Bhutan and Assam. More than 1,800 of them are in the forests of Assam's Kaziranga national park. Rising early, travelling on an elephant, I counted fifty-three rhinoceroses, thrillingly Jurassic. Some of them weigh two tonnes.

Thirty-five miles from Shillong, I came to Cherrapunji, reputedly the wettest place on earth when the south-west monsoon hits the hills. Local people refer to rain as slap, for the way it beats on the roof.

Scrambling up a hill, I came to a Christian cemetery where fading inscriptions on the gravestones evoked the struggles of Welsh missionaries in Victorian times. The Rev. Thomas Jones, who arrived in 1841, is honoured to this day by the million-strong Khasi tribe as the father of their written language, the saviour of their culture, the pioneering publisher of their literature. They sing their national anthem to the tune of *Hen Wlad Fy Nhadau*, an echo of eisteddfodau and rugby epics. The Khasis are a matrilineal people. Children take their mothers' names and family wealth is held in trust by the youngest daughter, one reason why Khasi women are so confident.

★

Gir Forest is an oasis in an arid region of Gujarat. It is the last and rather small refuge of the Indian lions. The encroachment of people and livestock threatens their survival. Forest dwellers poison lions because they eat their cattle. Pilgrims demand access to old temples in the forest, insisting on the right to worship in them and ignoring the authorities' attempts to limit their numbers. The respect accorded to pilgrims gives them considerable leverage.

I went for a drive in the jungle. A sign said: Lions Have Right of Way Here, but I entertained no hope of seeing one. It was the wrong time of the year and the grass cover was too high. The diesels were noisy and the guides, although enthusiastic, plainly knew little about the jungle. Still, the drive was enjoyable and the air good and there were plenty of birds to see.

When I returned from my drive, Mr Singh, the chef at the forest lodge, asked me if I had spotted a lion. When I shook my head, he said: 'Not spotted? I shall take you. I adore the jungle.'

In the late afternoon he presented himself as my guide and driver. He cut a dashing figure in his chef's uniform of white coat, chessboard trousers and black-and-white check neckerchief. He jumped into the car and drove off in high spirits, determined that I should spot a lion. It was his personal mission.

We drove this way and that, criss-crossing the jungle. 'This is good place,' Mr Singh said. 'Lion was seen here three days back.' Later, with less conviction, he paused at a ford and said: 'Lion is often here also.' The shadows lengthened, the sun sank and, with it, Mr Singh's spirits. It was quite dark before he admitted he was beaten.

'Today,' he concluded, 'there is not good spotting.'

At the hotel reception desk, there were expectant faces.

'Did you spot?'

'No, I did not spot.'

'Sir, come back when there is better spotting.'

'Yes,' said Mr Singh, brightening, 'I will take you and then you will spot.'

★

I drove to the national park at Kanha. The swathe of land in this part of Madhya Pradesh is called Kipling country because it is the setting of *The Jungle Book*, the stories of Mowgli and his extended family of forest creatures. The nearest Kipling got to it were glimpses of the countryside from a train during his last visit to India in 1891, a journey of four days and four nights from Ceylon to Lahore, in which he 'could not understand one word of the speech around me'. His imagination supplied all the colour.

A sign at the park entrance said Blow No Horn, an unusual instruction in India where the horn often appears to be wired to the throttle of every vehicle. Beside the gate stood a green-painted wooden office with a sign stating that it was the Doubt Clearance Cell. Inside, a forestry official in a khaki uniform was writing in a ledger.

'What is the Doubt Clearance Cell?' I asked.

'It is to clear up doubts. It is for answering questions, for assisting.'

'So you could tell me how many tigers there are in the national park?'

'Yes. More than one hundred are there.'

'Will the tigers survive?'

'Yes.'

'How do you know?'

'There is no doubt.'

Chapter 17

Mirrored mountains

From a distant minaret a muezzin called the drowsy from their dreams. Prayer, he chanted, is better than sleep. Before dawn cracked we crossed the lake in slender skiffs, boatmen spearing water with heart-shaped paddle blades. We were off to buy spices in the haggle of the water market.

In a lattice of canals and curtseying willows, we nosed into a flotilla of boats with plentiful cargoes of fruits and vegetables and saffron. The vale of Kashmir is eighty-five miles long, twenty-five wide, rich with apricots, cherries, peaches, pears, roses and jasmine. On the Dal lake near Srinagar we are a mile high, above the roasting plains and among glorious cedars, noble plane trees, blue pines and poplars. In the looking-glass lake we see the Himalayas. It has to be said, however, that India has squandered its assets in the forests.

I first travelled Kashmir in 1981, rode horses in the hills and walked for miles, watched craftsmen shape willow into cricket bats. I usually stayed in one of Mr Butt's traditional houseboats on the lake shore, wonderful with wood carving, chandeliers and vivid chintz. Most are blessed with whimsical names like Heaven's Tiger, Buckingham Palace, Neil Armstrong and Young Pinafore. The British first built these boats to evade a maharaja's edict forbidding foreigners owning land in Kashmir. 'Hello, my dear,' Mr Butt would say, and then show me his guest album of the stars who had stayed on his boats.

Kashmir lies where the frontiers of India, Pakistan, Afghanistan and China coincide. Akbar, the greatest Mogul emperor, seized it in the 1580s. His son loved wine and water gardens. Asked to name his last desire as he lay dying, he said: 'Only Kashmir.'

In the 1950s the historian Oskar Spate likened the story of Kashmir to the Happy Valley portrayed in *Rasselas*, Dr Johnson's warning against attractive but false recipes for happiness. 'However pleasant the prospects,' Spate wrote, 'the human history of the region has been, on the whole, vile.'

Sadness is beauty's companion. Bombs in Srinagar in 1988 started a war in which many thousands were killed.

In 1994, I went to Kashmir to report the kidnapping at gunpoint of two British trekkers, Kim Housego, aged sixteen, and David Mackie, who was thirty-six. The kidnappers were part of a Muslim group fighting Indian rule in Kashmir. I knew Kim's father, David. He had been a reporter on the *Financial Times*. I travelled with him and his wife as they toured the countryside appealing for information.

One afternoon someone slipped a note to David directing him to the town of Anantnag. I said I would go with him. It was a long drive. We met Dr Qasi Nisar, a respected cleric, who contacted the kidnappers. We waited with him in a house. After an hour, four masked men came in, two of them armed with Kalashnikovs. They shook hands with us. One spoke good English, his breath puffing out his black mask. He said the captives would be released and told us to wait for news in Srinagar. The men left quickly. Two days later Dr Nisar was shot dead. In the Kashmir snakepit it was hard to say who had killed him. A BBC reporter and I joined the large crowd at his funeral. Seventeen days after the kidnapping Kim and David were freed near Srinagar. They had been well treated.

I returned to Kashmir the following summer to report the abduction of five western tourists, all men. One escaped, one was beheaded and the others were presumed killed.

Srinagar's phones were as bad as ever. Every evening I left Ahdoo's hotel in Srinagar and walked half a mile to an office where there was a working telephone. It was dark. I had been warned that I should walk slowly in the middle of the empty street, shining a torch beam on my face to identify myself. Police cars full of armed men passed me slowly. At the office I made a call to London and dictated my story. I walked back to Ahdoo's, the torch beam on my face. Every morning a waiter brought me tea and toast and the four-page morning papers *Greater Kashmir* and *Mirror of Kashmir*, with their catalogues of killings. On my way to meet a friend one morning I passed a policeman stationed on a

157

crowded street corner. I heard a gunshot. The policeman died on the pavement.

Kashmir is the offspring of bitter divorce, the partition of India in 1947. To Pakistan's enduring fury, the larger and more desirable section of Kashmir became part of India. The 1965 war over Kashmir demonstrated that India's forces would always prevail. In six years, from 1995-2000, 15,000 people died in the Kashmir conflict. Many people felt that they had seen enough boys killed. There is a wish for a solution. The last time I went to Kashmir, a sign at Srinagar airport said: Welcome to the Paradise on Earth. Thousands of troops, gun emplacements and plenty of barbed wire reinforced the welcome. For old time's sake, I went to Ahdoo's for lunch. Things were looking up. We ate lotus cooked in yogurt.

India will never give up its portion of Kashmir to an independent Pakistan. The struggle for Kashmir is pointless and it cannot be won by arms. Even if all of Kashmir had been ceded to Pakistan in 1947, Pakistan would still have created a grievance, something to hate with. I always remember that long ago, as I sat on a houseboat veranda in Dal Lake, I felt the tremble of an earthquake, a single dark ripple on the moonlit water.

★

I had last been in Haiti in the final days of the dictator Baby Doc. I saw him fly into exile as people danced in delight. Hope rose as the charismatic priest-politician Jean-Bertrand Aristide was elected president, but army officers overthrew him and sent him into exile. Haiti returned to the old nightmare times with the thugs in charge.

In 1993 I went back to Oloffson's hotel, eerie in moonlight. Graham Greene would have jotted a note about the fretwork. Aubelin Jolicoeur was still there, as dapper as ever. This evening he wore a blazer and a paisley cravat. Oloffson's proprietor, Richard, an Italian–American, talked of Brown, the hotel's proprietor in *The Comedians*. 'I'm not like Brown,' he said, 'but, like him, I love the place. It's a piece of history. I like the sort of people who stay here. If the military stop running the country, we'll get democracy and I'll get tourists. If not, I'll get journalists.'

The slaves of Haiti overthrew their French masters in 1804 and declared a republic. Blacks were 95 per cent of the population, mulattos five per cent. Papa Doc, the tyrant father of Baby Doc, invented the Tontons Macoutes. They killed tens of thousands of people. The Macoutes did not vanish with Baby Doc. They re-emerged as thugs called Attachés.

I rented a car when I arrived in Port-au-Prince. It shuddered badly and the windscreen was cracked. Because Creole is the only language most Haitians know, I found a Creole guide. He and I drove into the city. Another reporter came with us. I saw a woman attacked. An Attaché beat her on her back and shoulders with a stave. He turned and started attacking an old man in the same way. People fled, leaping over piles of garbage, skidding on fruit skins. More thugs appeared. We drove to a bus station. In a moment we were surrounded by Attachés, four men waving pistols and yelling.

Their leader had his finger on the trigger and pushed his screaming face into mine. He was furious. He saw my camera on the back seat and tore the film from it. There was a moment when we seemed to be in the balance. The four thugs spat and screamed abuse, guns close to our heads. At last, they ordered us into the clapped-out car. We drove out of the bus station, shaken. That evening a storm came down the mountain and lashed against the hotel. A car stopped close by and shots were fired. The ceiling fan turned the thick air. In the small hours, I heard gunshots and dogs barking.

★

At a time when Rajiv Gandhi was learning and pondering his new way of life he came to my home in Delhi to talk informally to a group of foreign correspondents. I saw him again when he was campaigning in an election.

After his mother's death during the Sikh crisis in 1984, Rajiv was quickly sworn in as prime minister. He was not a man of strong political ideas and experience. He rode a wave of goodwill, the Nehru effect, as the new man at the top of the family business. But many thought him inexperienced and doubted he was tough enough to deal with his enemies and his mistakes.

In 1986 I interviewed Rajiv at his room in the parliament in Delhi. He had been leading the country for twenty months. He smiled and said that being prime minister of India was often worse than flying through turbulence. 'There is sometimes tremendous slack in the controls, the inertial forces are incredible, and the passengers are very impatient.' One difficulty, he said, was that India's economic progress had raised expectations. But he added that India's strength was its resilience.

The Nehru family, he said, had led India for all but four of its thirty-nine years of independence. 'The greatest achievement is to have maintained a democratic and united country. Not many newly-independent countries have done well on that score.'

I returned to India to report the election of May 1991. At that time of the year the atmosphere was as hot as a rotisserie. I started in the city of Aligarh on the Jumna river, writing that 'the sun rises with its promise of fresh pain'.

This was an election full of significance, the stakes high, 9,000 candidates charging to and fro in convoys of cars. Some of them descended from helicopters in storms of dust, like gods. Garish portraits of party leaders, five times life-size, bestrode tall buildings. The politicians ranged from the high-minded to the graspingly unsavoury and the toughs. A villager in his seventies spoke feelingly to me: 'I learned English in British times, so you will understand when I say that these politicians are buggers, sir; buggers, vagabonds and thieves.'

The election was taking place forty-four years after independence. An era had all but ended. Nehru, the first prime minister, raised as an English Edwardian gentleman, had little stomach for the political venality and rough-housing beneath the crust. Indira, his daughter, had no illusions. She split and weakened the Congress party. She declared the emergency in which many journalists and others were jailed. Her cruel son Sanjay persecuted the poor. Nehru's vision of a secular society of Hindus and Muslims had all but vanished. He once said that the people of India were the substance of India. His daughter, however, said: 'India is Indira.'

I left the sweaty excitement of Aligarh and travelled to Mysore, planning to watch Rajiv campaigning a couple of days later in Madras. Around 10.20 in the evening he appeared at a rally near the city. A young woman moved forward as if to touch his feet in respect. As she did so, she detonated the explosives strapped to her body and killed Rajiv and fourteen other people. She was a Tamil Tiger. The foreign desk of *The Daily Telegraph* called me in Mysore and asked me to write 1,000 words within forty-five minutes.

'I cannot imagine that many people slept in India last night,' I began. 'The news flashed from the foothills of the Himalayas to the beaches of Comorin, from the desert in the west, to the jungle in the east. A vast country, already bewildered, in the middle of the most crucial election of the forty-four years of independence, was jerked into shocking wakefulness.'

Rajiv's wife Sonia and his daughter Priyanka flew to Madras and brought his body back to Delhi. I saw it on a bier scattered with jasmine and marigolds in the house which had been Nehru's home. Sonia sat nearby, composed, wearing a white sari, the emblem of mourning. The body was carried through the petal-strewn avenues of Delhi, watched by immense crowds. This last journey took three hours. Rajiv's son Rahul lit the pyre on the bank of the Jumna river.

Chapter 18

The white stones

In 1993, 1994 and 1995, I reported solemn ceremonies in Belgium and France, the Netherlands, Poland and Japan. These marked, first of all, the end of the first world war, then the Allied liberation of France and the battle at Arnhem, the end of Hitler's Reich, the Allied victory in Europe and the defeat of Japan.

In November 1993, the seventy-fifth anniversary of the armistice of 1918, the direct human link to the great war was all but severed. The elderly men with whom I travelled from London to Ypres and the immense military cemeteries on the gentle slopes of the battlefield were the last of the last. Yet, still, they retained a soldierly bearing and raised their chins at the sound of bugles. At Tyne Cot, the largest British cemetery, where 11,500 men are buried, I talked to Donald Hodge. He was almost ninety-nine, but in his dignified manner, the way he held himself, there was still something to see of the tall young man who came here to fight.

'I'm thinking,' he said, 'about the boys I knew who didn't make it. I mourn, of course, but I remember that laughter was never far from tears.'

In Ypres Reginald Glenn, 100 years old, delivered the exhortation 'We will remember them' in a ringing Yorkshire voice. 'We don't come just to look at graves,' he said, 'we think of our friends as they were, young men and joking.'

As we talked, I looked into the eyes of these men who on these battlefields had squinted down their rifle sights, had seen their friends fall. Later that day I saw them march to the Menin Gate memorial in Ypres. The band played *Where Are the Boys of the Old Brigade,* and there they were, at the front, saluting, straight. The very last of the boys.

★

The men who came to Normandy in June 1994 were making a pilgrimage to their own youth. They trod the beaches and went to the streets and hedgerows where their friends died. They remembered the bloodied sea, the falling waves washing the dead. They were still calling themselves Shorty, Chalky, Jock, Taffy and Paddy. They looked around and asked: 'Where's old Ginger? Where's Lofty?' They joshed each other about their moustaches and balding heads. More than a few had a limp and a walking stick. They wore berets and kilts, blazers and glinting medals. Small things, a snatch of Glenn Miller, sand dunes and the smell of fresh bread unlocked a memory. This was the fiftieth anniversary of D-Day. The Queen came. There would never be anything like it again.

At the great parade men slotted their hands under the elbows of comrades whose marching was not quite what it had once been. A man talked me through the fighting at Pegasus Bridge. He had helped to capture it fifty years before. Just ordinary blokes, they tell you. Old boys, old boys. They walked on the beach and left their footprints in the sand, where they had left them fifty years before.

★

Beneath the trees of Oosterbeek the fallen acorns lay. The oak trees stood as timeless honour guards. Their leaves whispered. Three miles from Arnhem, Oosterbeek was at the heart of the fighting in September 1944. In the war cemetery here lie 1,755 soldiers. At the fiftieth anniversary service, the crowd assembled to salute their courage. Old comrades were here wearing their paratroopers' maroon berets, there were proud widows and children and the ordinary people of Holland, humble and grateful, always loyal in their remembrance. Veterans marched to lay wreaths at the memorial. The medals on their blazers sounded a gentle tintinnabulation. At a signal children in their hundreds turned to face the white headstones and each one placed a posy.

The bold ambition of the operation, called Market Garden, was to secure a bridge across the Rhine. It failed, and many were killed.

After the ceremony, veterans sat in a café and reminisced. 'See there? That crossroads? That's where I was captured.' Another pointed and said: 'Just over there, that's where I was wounded.'

★

In Auschwitz you forget nothing. You cannot conceal even the smallest memory. Fifty years after the Allies liberated it, in January 1945, this monstrous death camp still disturbs and makes you feel contaminated. There is nothing for your comfort.

It remains disquieting and inescapable, a pit of human malevolence. In the ruined gas chamber, a large cold room, your footfall echoes. It is not only the chill that makes you shiver. A single candle flickers, a wintry light falls from a hole in the ceiling through which gas once flowed. The adjoining room is dominated by red brick ovens where bodies were burnt. The harsh name of Auschwitz represents more than the largest Nazi extermination camp. It also speaks of the wider horror of the Holocaust. Nine-tenths of the one and a half million people killed here were Jewish. Between Block 10 and Block 11 is the death wall where thousands of people were marched out in pairs to be shot. The photographs show the pitiful portrayed by the pitiless, defiled and helpless men and women. It is not possible to forget their gaunt and haunting faces. You will see them again. You cannot forget the mounds of prisoners' belongings, the heaps of shoes and spectacles. And the baby clothes. Dr Joseph Mengele worked here. A prisoner who escaped Auschwitz watched an SS man kill children aged four and five. One of these children kissed the man's boot. The SS man killed him all the same.

I met a Hungarian Jewish woman, aged seventy, who arrived here in July 1944. Those fit enough to work were ordered to the right, those to be gassed to the left: this woman and her sister were assigned to slave labour, the rest of her family sent to death.

'This is the second time I have been back,' she told me. 'I have come because I want to tell people what happened so that it is never forgotten.'

During my second day at Auschwitz, I heard that there was a crude sign by the roadside: Juden Raus, it said. So the virus is not completely dead.

★

The American B-29 *Enola Gay* dropped its four-ton atomic bomb on Hiroshima at 8.15 on 6 August 1945. On that warm Monday morning children were heading to school and adults to work. The bomb fell for forty-three seconds and detonated at 1,900 feet. Every survivor remembered the incandescent flash and monstrous roar. Two hundred thousand people died.

From the cinders, Hiroshima's leaders created a city devoted to peace. It is the home of more than a million people and full of the energy of the young generations. The horror of 1945, however, is not concealed. Fifty years on, Japan remains haunted by Hiroshima. Hideous photographs and shocking films, shredded clothing and melted objects, are permanent witnesses. I listened to the narratives of storytellers who related what they experienced. One of them, Mrs Iwamoto, gathered thirty-five children around her and described the collapse of her school, a mile from the centre of the explosion. The city was a sea of flame. Her arms, face and feet were burned. Children stared at their hands which had fallen apart. Her mother found her and spread mashed cucumber on her wounds. She recovered, married, had two children. She tells her story.

Everyone, every visitor, can see and hear the events of 1945. Japan is tormented by Hiroshima. Many believe the bombing was a slaughter of the innocent, that Japan was a victim and should not apologize for atrocities, that theirs was not a dishonourable cause.

A poll, however, showed a majority in favour of apology. On the eve of the fiftieth anniversary a former Japanese fighter pilot said that had America not dropped the bomb many more people would have died. 'It was absurd for Japan to take on the Americans,' he said. 'The stupid men running our navy and army should have surrendered much earlier.'

Sixty thousand people attended the memorial in Hiroshima on 6 August. At 8.15, they fell silent. A child and an adult grasped a stout wooden beam and pushed it against the rim of the Peace Bell. The deep and solemn note resonated in the warm air. The mayor of Hiroshima apologized for Japan's wartime aggression, the suffering it had inflicted. The shimmering haze of the Flame of Peace was a reminder that, fifty years before, there was a flash brighter than the sun.

Chapter 19

May days

Max Hastings left the editor's chair of *The Daily Telegraph* in 1995. 'Ten years is enough,' he said. This made me think. It was time for a change. As a roving foreign correspondent, the job he offered me in 1986, I had enjoyed ten crowded years of travelling and writing around the world, including more than two years as Moscow correspondent in the dramatic Gorbachev years. Max himself described the pleasures of writing for a newspaper which accommodated a great range of essays and features on human affairs. I felt the same way. For a decade I wrote news and features for the main pages, the foreign pages, features, magazines, book reviews and travel. That followed my seventeen years of reporting for *The Times* including the three-year postings in India and New York.

After another spell in India, and then in Israel, I left *The Daily Telegraph* in 1996 to be a freelance. I wrote from America, Canada, Australia, Russia, China, Africa, India, Pakistan and the Caribbean. In 1997 I reflected on the fiftieth anniversary of the independence of India and Pakistan. Some of my travels and research among historical sites, battlefields, buildings, libraries and journeys in wild places contributed to two books: *Cobra Road*, a journey from the Khyber to the southern tip of India at Cape Comorin; and *Conquerors of Time*, an account of exploration and invention in the eighteenth and nineteenth centuries. I also had the pleasure of leading four tour groups in India, and delivering the daily pre-dinner lecture.

During my fifties, and to my surprise, I also fell into television. I wrote and presented a series of half-hour programmes called *Wild Tracks*. Wil Aaron was the director, a noted film maker, a lover of history and addicted to books. He had worked for the BBC's *24 Hours* in Vietnam and the Middle East. Indeed, he had directed the young Max Hastings. Menna Richards, the director of programmes at HTV

Cymru Wales, brought us together. *Wild Tracks* was transmitted at the peak time of 7.30 pm and ran for fourteen years.

Mostly we filmed in May when light sparkled and bluebells were bluer. As a foreign correspondent I had usually travelled alone, so that working in a television team was a new and rewarding experience. Wil Aaron planted his imprimatur on the programmes through his reconnaissance of history and landscape. He revelled in the stories and marked his Ordnance Survey with compelling views. He also had the knack of finding sunshine. We made programmes in every part of Wales, from Anglesey to the Severn Sea. In each series of six we filmed two in north Wales, two in the middle and two in the south. Each episode took four days to shoot.

Along the way we unearthed tellers of tales in the Chaucer fashion: a handy historian, a horse-whisperer, a jolly wife, a postwoman, a seaside metal detectorist, a calligrapher, a cartographer, a vintner, a coracle-fisher, a blue-scarred coalminer, a female blacksmith. Often, when we set up the camera to interview a farmer, his border collies would arrive to cock their ears and listen carefully to what he had to say.

For me there were arts to be learned. As presenter and writer, I had to speak pithily, not hurriedly, gently off the cuff. There could be no autocue. Speaking to the camera, I had to squeeze words into a simple essence. Nothing could be wasted. I wrote my brief lines on postcards and whittled them into shape. Then I learned them, giving no appearance of having memorized them. In the last stages, in the dubbing suite, when the film had been cut and polished, I tailored my commentary words to the spaces. Wil had ensured during the filming that my pronunciation of Welsh place names would please the most prickly of professors.

We mined the raw material of landscape, legends, history and stories. Soon we went to Snowdon. It owed some of its popularity to Napoleon Bonaparte. The wars with France placed large areas of Europe out of bounds and stopped the grand continental tours so popular with young British gentlemen. Looking for other sensations, they soon discovered Snowdonia's alpine grandeur, romantic atmosphere and melodrama. They were enchanted, too, by the young women of Snowdonia.

'Pretty pouting lips,' wrote one.

'My Welsh beauty of Snowdon,' said another.

Writing so lyrically of embonpoint, necks and curves, these explorers needed a cold bath at day's end. Still, such young men were a source of income to farmers and mountain guides who took visitors to the summit. Some of these were celebrities. Robert Edwards, for example, advertised himself as 'Guide-General and Magnificent Expounder of all the natural curiosities of north Wales.'

On a Snowdon cliff, I rendezvoused with an abseiling botanist, a television natural. She showed me the Snowdon lily, one of Europe's rarest flowers. Its yellow petals, the size of a sixpence, were sheltered by a rock and bloomed for only for two weeks. I climbed a cliff rope to enter a Gower cave. We filmed in a darkened house filled with bats. I paddled a coracle over the Teifi. I fought a fear of heights to walk across the Pontcysyllte viaduct and did it twice more to please the cameraman, a speck far below. We all wriggled on our stomachs and conquered claustrophobia to enter a wonderful cave and film inside it. In a Monmouthshire wood I slid into what seemed to be a foxhole. It was the concealed entrance to a dank chamber where, in the 1940s, local men with guns and grenades readied for desperate battle should Nazi invaders come. They would have been the last line of defence and would not have survived. We also crossed a meadow and disappeared down a ladder into a concrete chamber. Here, in the event of a nuclear war, men would have monitored the effects of atomic bombs.

I walked in Anglesey fields where in 1910 the actor Robert Loraine, London heart-throb, made aviation history. Out of fuel, he crash-landed here, repaired the plane and crashed again. Rebuilding it, he saw to his horror a pig eating the fabric of a wing. Taking off, he crashed once more. He loaded the aircraft onto a wagon and repaired it at Holyhead. He took off, aiming to be the first to fly to Dublin. He landed in the sea a mile from the Irish coast and swam ashore. Still, he reached London in time to take the stage at the Haymarket in a play called *The Man from the Sea*. In the first world war he flew as a fighter pilot.

Of course, we worked in many churches. We filmed some of the murder stones, too. It was the custom in parts of Wales, when a murderer had not been brought to justice, to record that fact on the victim's tombstone and to add that the killer would be punished in this world or the next. Jane Lewis's stone at Tonyrefail says that she was killed 'by a cruel hand, unavenged ... God lives, revenge is his'.

The Pryce family tomb, at Newtown in the Severn valley, tells that Sir John Pryce, born in 1698, so mourned his first wife that he had her embalmed and placed by his bed. The second Lady Pryce was similarly embalmed to rest on the bed's other side. Sir John's third wife refused to share the room with her two stuffed predecessors; and good Sir John acknowledged that in the matter of wives in a bedroom three was a crowd.

Near Denbigh we told the story of the remarkable Catrin of Berain, a most lovable woman of the late sixteenth century. Married four times, she was called 'the mother of Wales' for her niche in so many family trees. At her first husband's funeral she politely refused Maurice Wynn's proposal of marriage. She had already accepted the proposal of Sir Richard Clough, who was escorting her into the church. She murmured to Wynn, however, that he could count on being her number three; and after Clough's death four years later he became so. In his will, Clough paid her a loving tribute. 'I have found my wife so good, honest and friendly during my life I desire all my friends to love and honour her after my death for she is of honesty and lovingness and worthy to marry any King.'

In woods beside the Wye we found a mysterious hole twenty feet deep, a remnant of the obsession of Orville Ward Owen, a doctor from Detroit. He believed Francis Bacon wrote Shakespeare's plays and had hidden the manuscripts in sixty-six iron boxes in the Wye valley. In 1909, handsomely financed by his backers, Owen dug for three months near Chepstow castle. Finding nothing he concluded that the boxes lay in the riverbed and hired engineers to dam and excavate it. Defeated, he went home to America in 1911. His disciples, however, returned in the 1920s, raised the Stars and Stripes and dug deep holes in the woods of Wye. Of Bacon, however, they found no sign.

At Llaneilian church in Anglesey we filmed the stout timber dog tongs. Shepherds used to take their dogs to morning service. If the sermon were long they encouraged the dogs to fight and bark. To stop this uproar churchwardens reached for the tongs, grasped the dogs by the neck and threw them into the churchyard. In Ceredigion, I saw a family pew which had the luxury of a fireplace. When the matriarch tired of a sermon she rattled a poker in the grate, driving the preacher from the pulpit.

A woman who had lived most of her life in Laugharne told us that she had known Dylan Thomas well. She cut his hair before he left for America in 1953. When she had finished snipping he looked in the mirror and said: 'Lovely, it'll last me a lifetime.' The trip ended in his death in New York.

In 1770 the Reverend William Gilpin published a study of the River Wye and advocated that visitors should view it through his 'rules of picturesque beauty'. Good ruins, he thought, enhanced a landscape and he was satisfied that the remnants of Tintern abbey were especially picturesque. Some visitors thought Tintern's ruins not gloomy enough and wished they would inspire a little more melancholy.

The small and charming town of Montgomery seems to be as comfortable as an old tweed jacket. Its square is large. Its Elizabethan and Georgian houses are built to a medieval street pattern. It seems to some visitors that it is a town stolen from England and dragged across the border. The old school log book, displayed in the town museum, records that 'today the ink froze in the inkwells', and 'I had to punish Charlie Jones for pinching Amy Sloan while trying to stuff de-worming powder down her throat.'

We filmed at Poyston, the Pembrokeshire home of General Thomas Picton. He was the most senior officer killed at the Battle of Waterloo in 1815, the best of Wellington's generals. His horse survived and was brought to Poyston to spend the rest of its days in a meadow. After it died its skull was interred beneath the living room floor. 'Would you like to see it?' the owner said. I helped him to roll back the carpet. In a dramatic ending to the programme, he lifted a hatch in the floorboards to reveal the horse's skull. There was something compelling in this. Funerals of kings and generals have traditionally included a horse with an empty saddle. In its way, the Poyston skull suggested an equine tribute to a warrior.

In the Vale of Clwyd we filmed the birthplace of David Samwell, a parson's son, who became a naval surgeon and sailed in the *Resolution* on the last of Captain Cook's epic voyages. He was close by when Cook was hacked to death in Hawaii in February 1779. His account of the voyage reported Cook's tragic end in detail. With Iolo Morganwg, David Samwell was a founder of the Gorsedd, the Bards of Britain, in 1792. We also told the story of Henry Morton Stanley, born in Denbigh, who in Africa found fame, and Dr Livingstone, in 1871.

In Wales the stories bloom forever. I liked the fables as well as the documented history. We had the voices of a storytelling people and the jigsaw of varied landscapes, a panorama of vignettes and watercolours. In its craggy way it can look like a fortress, forbidding as well as grand. In all of our eighty-four *Wild Tracks* programmes we never tired of the look of the land, always found Wales speaking eloquently and entertainingly for itself.

Later I worked on two series of *Sea Stories*, maritime histories of Wales, for the BBC. I wrote and presented stories for the BBC from the archives of the National Library of Wales, and several series of programmes for ITV Wales, including a profile of two Tenby artists, Gwilym Prichard and his wife Claudia Williams, a delightful couple. For the BBC I also told the story of the Davies sisters, Gwendoline and Margaret, and their remarkable art collection.

Chapter 20

A go on the elephant

Perhaps my Piscean fishes steered me to the sea. I remember an open boat at Southsea, my father jumping onto the beach to whisk me from my mother, passing me across the gunwale, hauling himself aboard as the oarsmen dug the wave. In early days I sailed an old gunter dinghy, restored a canoe to cross the Solent, crewed cross-Channel to learn more ropes, read Slocum, Gerbault and Tilman, saw the Hiscocks, Chichester, Rose, Villiers, Knox-Johnston and talked to Herbert Hasler, RM, who led the Cockleshell Heroes and later inspired Atlantic voyagers. For years, my friend Ronald Faux and I have sailed among Scotland's islands. I also sail with Luke Powell, oakstruck traditionalist, builder of lovely Victorian pilot cutters. I cannot resist the ferries: Sydney, Hong Kong, New York, the Brahmaputra, the Andamans, Shanghai and Gosport, and the Bombay boats biffing their way to Elephanta Island.

★

For a half-asleep second, I did not know where I was. I became aware of scampering squirrels and chipmunks, bustling warblers and raucous jays. I was on the island, in my sleeping bag at the edge of dawn, the tent picturesquely frosted. I opened the zip. Sunlight lit the glades. In this vast outback, no human sound or engine disturbed the tranquil lakes: there were no buildings or roads. Our only means of travel was our slim and silent canoe drawn up above the little beach.

Our bag of food dangled from a high pine branch beyond the reach of black bears. Brian, my guide, said bears steered away from people, though they might nose around at night. He'd met a few troublesome ones in his time. 'They can sense fear,' he said, 'so you have to show authority.' He pitched our tents thirty yards apart. I resolved to leave the bears to him.

I had canoed in this great wilderness twenty-five years before and had promised myself a return trip. I drove from Minneapolis to the Lake Superior shore, turned off at Grand Marais and headed for the immensity of the Boundary Waters. In the eighteenth and nineteenth centuries voyageurs exploring thousands of miles of this virgin waterland established the canoe as an emblem of Canada's romance and mythology.

When Brian became a guide, he and his wife moved into a timber cabin without electricity or piped water. He fished for bass and trout, hunted his permitted allowance of deer and trained huskies for sled racing. When terrorists smashed the towers in New York, he was canoeing these wilderness waters and heard nothing about it for a week.

We paddled and portaged, carrying the canoe across the islands through the woods. Entrances to portages are not signposted and are sometimes difficult to see. 'It's a wilderness,' Brian said, 'you need to look after yourself and read a map.'

The portages were measured in old-fashioned rods. The exercise books at my primary school had handy weights and measures on the covers, so I knew that a rod was five and a half yards and portage of sixty-eight rods was 374 yards. We paddled our way from island to island. The canoe was light enough for Brian to carry on his shoulders.

Towards the end of the afternoon, we reached an islet and set up camp and gathered firewood. The park provides only two services, a fire grill and a small latrine without walls.

As the light faded and the air grew chilly, we lit the fire and sipped Brian's bourbon. He sizzled potatoes and onions in bacon fat and cooked two of his cedar-smoked steaks. We ate the same meal beneath the stars every evening. It was easier that way. We washed up carefully, hauled our rubbish high, left no specks for inquisitive bears, and talked as the logs crackled. Next day, after coffee and pancakes, we paddled and portaged, fished and ate lunch, and watched otters playing in the sun.

Brian listed some observations of his clients. Although men were often lazy, he had noticed that a woman's presence drove them to work harder. 'Kids aged fifteen to nineteen and people over sixty are the best clients for me,' he said. 'They're the ones who are keen to learn.'

ʌ

On the day I started work at the *Evening News*, I knew little but my resolve to be a reporter. I had no doubt that this was my fortunate first step; and this was the life for me. I bought a book published in wartime to learn the history of the press. A good press, it said, was as essential to a country's wellbeing as good government. Its function was to portray life. Nine-tenths of Britain read a daily paper, even more on Sunday. I embarked on a life of portraying life, the collective effort, the love of news, the thrill of the story. Months later, upstairs on a bus, I saw that everyone was reading the Late Extra edition of the *Evening News*. If only they would hurry up and turn to the next page they would see the interesting court case I had covered that morning.

Journalism put a shine on the blue suit my father bought me. I now typed and knew shorthand. I was young, inexperienced, clumsy, but older hands taught me interviewing skills, how to listen, to develop a good telephone manner. We all grew up with the red sentry box, the K2 telephone kiosk designed by Sir Giles Gilbert Scott in 1926, inspired by a Regency mausoleum. It was a lighthouse, an office, a shelter from the rain. Most of us started on the newspaper at the age of sixteen. But times were changing, and I remember having the *Evening News*'s first university graduate pointed out to me, rather as if he were a rare beast, like an okapi.

In time I enjoyed the excitement and friendships of Fleet Street life and learned something of what Keith Waterhouse described in his book as *The Theory and Practice of Lunch*. I was fortunate. Both in my years at *The Times* and *The Daily Telegraph*, I was a foreign correspondent. The foreign news editor of *The Times* described the posting to India as 'a go on the elephant'. I was indebted to him and to others for the experiences I had abroad, the opportunity to learn countries, people and their histories. I was fortunate to live in Delhi, New York and Moscow, to have the company of British, Indian, Pakistani, French, Australian and American colleagues, to be able to travel and explore, to pursue and come back with the stories. I remain as I began, a devoted newspaper reader. I read just as my mother and father did in the age before television. The enthusiasm for journalism that propelled my love for it remains much the same today.

★

In Shanghai, as my guide for the day, genial Henry Hong wore a crisp shirt with his pressed shorts and gleaming white trainers. Cool and neat is Shanghai's summer style. When we met, Henry stared at my feet and laughed with delight. 'Leather shoes in hot weather,' he chuckled, 'proper British gentleman!' He took me to lunch in a smart restaurant. 'See our fashion-conscious ladies,' he said, with a proprietorial wave of his hand, 'how good they look.' And so they did. Shanghai's people have no doubt that they are number one in everything. Their women, they insist, are the most attractive in the country. Henry and I watched as their cups were constantly refreshed by a tea-boy. He carried a teapot with a thin spout three feet long. With unerring aim, he sent a splashless jet of tea fifteen inches long from spout to cup. Henry ordered lunch. A quivering fish, taken alive from a tank, was sliced and stir-fried and on our plates in two minutes. All the male lunchers had chopsticks in one hand and cellphones in the other. Henry pointed out that the new-fangled cellphones were status symbols, and, of course, many of them were fakes. But no one would dare to appear in public without one.

Henry showed me the skyscrapers. They seemed to be growing by the hour in the world's greatest assembly of construction cranes. A hotel manager said with a smile: 'What you write today is out of date tomorrow.' The Shanghai building frenzy was accompanied by a terrible outbreak of karaoke. Henry took me to a new restaurant area where we had a beer and a spring onion pancake. 'You can get anything you want here,' he said proudly. We watched a man put a snake into a bag. Presumably he was going to cook it at home.

The best place for contemplating the city and its people is the Bund, the broad embankment beside the Huangpu river. Here you can see China's grandest paseo, Shanghai's favourite meeting place. There was no graceless jogging. I was impressed by the polish and poise of people conducting their balletic exercises in squares and streets, painting the air with their fingers, describing parentheses with long curved swords. I saw some young women walking swiftly backwards as an exercise in balance. Then I was impressed when I saw some spry elderly men with briefcases doing the same. The people were absorbed in their catlike exercises. I admired their studied dignity as they waltzed to the

175

reedy sound of a cassette player, their own molecule of peace amid the fever of the city. I paid a small fee to walk the pathways and rockeries through The Hall of Observing in Quietness and into the Corridor of Gradually Entering Wonderland.

★

Bombay always surprises. Walking the streets one day I heard a pillow fluffer twanging his bow. He earned his living opening up mattresses and pillows and, with his bow, separating hard and matted lumps of cotton. Then he teased the stuffing until it was fluffy once more, ensuring sweeter dreams.

Chapter 21

Dateline dispatches

Fairbanks, Alaska, 2006. Mary was a musher in Alaska, dotty about dogs. 'Can you howl?' she asked nicely. I said I hadn't howled for years, but I'd be happy to try. She had invited me to dinner at her log house near Fairbanks and told me all about falling in love with Alaska, then falling in love with mushing: racing dog teams through the snow. She had competed in the classic long-distance races and was the first woman to complete the annual Iditarod race, 1,200 miles from Anchorage to Nome. The Iditarod commemorates the heroic five-day dash of 1925 when relays of sled drivers carried serum to save diphtheria-stricken children in Nome. These epic races celebrate the era when dog teams were the only means of hauling supplies in winter. Dog sleds carried mail in Alaska until 1962. These days sled racing is big on television and in the papers.

Mary trains her sled dogs from puppies. 'Pedigree dogs are no use at all. They lack stamina and character.' She camps during her frequent winter trips in the wilds. Naturally she cooks the dogs' dinners first and settles them on snow mats. Only then does she make her own meal inside her tent, which is fitted with a chimney. Mushers work to their own secret dog dinner recipes. Musher comes from the French, marchez. 'Mushers,' said Mary, 'never say mush to the dogs. They call out gee, meaning right, and haw, meaning left.

Mary took me out to see her dogs in their quarters. It was a lovely darkless time of the year when the sun sets late and rises early. Here we raised our faces and howled a wolfish serenade. Mary's dogs howled a response. Alaska is full of surprises. How often have you howled a lullaby to a team of sled dogs?

Alaska means the great land in the Aleut language. Alaskans refer to the rest of the United States as The Outside. Their average age is twenty-seven. They stomp about in rude health and the men grow thick beards over plaid wool shirts. Half of the population is spread thinly over the vastness. Air travel is the only practical way to reach most of it and a large number of Alaskans have a pilot's licence, six times the national average. The other half of the population live in the ugly sprawl of Anchorage, a city with seventeen taxidermists. The great public debate is between Boomers who want Alaska opened up for its mineral wealth and Greenies who want the wilderness protected.

In two trips I saw quite a lot of Alaska. There is much more to see. George, a former miner, asked me if I would like to visit a gold mine. He drove me to a hillside wooden cottage where he grew up. He opened a stout door at the back of the kitchen and there it was: the cool and dripping goldmine his father had dug in the 1930s. 'Dad went through that door every morning,' George said. 'Mom heard the dynamite explosions and hoped for the best.'

Much of the romance and assertiveness of Alaska is squeezed into the slogan on the licence plates: Alaska the Last Frontier. Two of the most popular books are a thick volume of grizzly bear stories and a log cabin building manual. Many pioneers arrive to live a log cabin dream. To their dismay, they find parking tickets on their windscreens.

Up in the mountains a group of us put on crampons and hiked over a glacier. At the end of the trip I thanked the guide. 'Don't mention it,' he said, 'with your accent you raised the tone of the whole expedition.'

★

Falkland Islands, 1989. Falkland islanders always referred to those seventy-five days of invasion and fighting in 1982 as the Conflict. In its aftermath, they felt vindicated. Argentina's cabal of ruthless generals was humbled.

But the war was not the end of the matter. There remained the riddle of the Falkland Islands, the postage-stamp English parish at the earth's ends. Before the junta's invasion it was withering away, too small to possess all the brain, let alone the sinew, to handle growth: not enough young men or women, not enough education, not enough outsiders. When they looked at their school photographs, they saw that many of their classmates had quit, to live in Australia, New Zealand and Britain, to escape the rundown and feudalistic colony.

The British rescue and feat of arms in 1982 did not settle the inherent ambiguities and ambivalence in the Falklanders' situation. Three hundred miles off Patagonia they earnestly wished to be Little England Beyond the Seas. And, understandably, they also yearned for a South American aspect to their lives and horizons, to be able to stretch their legs and imaginations in Chile and Uruguay and, a more distant dream, in a renewed and reformed Argentina, too.

And what changes they had witnessed. Before the invaders came, the Falklands seemed a bit of unfinished imperial business, a fading colony about to be sold up the rio by the British.

Yet the confrontation between the junta on one hand, and the British forces and Margaret Thatcher on the other, led to transformation. At the time I visited the islands, they were a South Atlantic Klondike. The unemployment rate was zero. 'Anyone with more than one leg qualifies for a job,' I was told. Contract workers, mostly from Britain, were responding to the lure of good money and the prospect of adventure. They were building roads, houses and a telephone system and working in the busy docks.

I stayed in Stanley, the capital, for a few days, a place full of Land Rovers. On Sunday I called at a raucous pub. It was open only for sixty minutes, strictly enforced, the Falklands Glory Hour. There was barely room in this crush to raise a glass. Stevedores, sailors and shearers pressed on skivvies, navvies, engineers and entrepreneurs. Some had beer cans tucked under their epaulettes and perched on their hats. There were Greeks, Japanese, Englishmen, Irishmen, Scotsmen, Welshmen and, of course, Falklanders.

The magic ingredient in all this, the gold in the gold rush, was supplied by squid, the gold calamari, the hitherto unexploited Falklands treasure. Squidivorous Spaniards, Koreans, Japanese and Taiwanese, using trawlers and electronic rods and lines called squid-jiggers, contributed a large part of the £16 million paid for licence fees in the new 150-mile radius Falklands fishing zone.

The former Falklands treasurer told me that in forty years the islands' revenue had increased from £100,000, mostly from stamps and wool, to £35 million. Out in the sound fishing boats were unloading into mother ships. There were 200 vessels at work. With this wealth,

Falklanders feel they count for something after years of economic slump. Many believe that the population must continue to grow. Some think they might become a minority in their own land.

Reminders of Britain are everywhere in English rural scenes, pictures of the Queen and teaspoons from Torquay. A good number of settlers are escapees from Britain and enjoy hard work and self-sufficiency in an exhilarating landscape. Many of the large ranches, with their tied cottages and the company store, have been divided into smaller farms.

I flew in a Britten-Norman Islander to Port Howard in West Falkland, a traditional large farm with a trout stream and a school, the whole place as idyllic as a butter commercial. I flew on to Sea Lion Island, population eight, where there's a tourist lodge. There was also company nearby, access to the gentle penguins and elephant seals, huge old gents twenty feet long and four tons, belching on the beach, scratching, rumbling and roaring.

Some people talk nostalgically of the slow old days. Others are the frontiersmen of the faster new days, hoping for a Falklands future for their children. Meanwhile they are comforted by the military presence, the fighter planes, living behind the shield.

★

Pangnirtung, Baffin Island, 1988. At home I have a pale blue print of Inuit people, also known as Eskimos, hunting on the seashore. I bought it from the artist in his studio. It reminds me of his people's determination to survive, that they are hunters or they are nothing.

Their village is Pangnirtung, Pang for short, a settlement of more than 1,000 people, 95 per cent Eskimo, on a spectacular Baffin Island fjord. I went there to write about them and stayed in their small hotel. Pang's artistic tradition began when whalers gave pencils to Eskimos. Printing, weaving and carving help to sustain them.

The print tells me, too, that they have learnt how to survive among white men in the white world. The heart of the village is the Hudson's Bay Company store, the commercial force in the Canadian north for more than three centuries, crammed with the essentials of Arctic life:

rifles, knives, mittens, thick socks, axes and fish hooks, ropes and chains, snowmobiles and outboards, down-filled parkas.

Mothers pick up free recipes at the store, printed in Eskimo and English, suggesting caribou curry. Babies peep from the pouches on their backs. A true motif for the modern Arctic is not the igloo or the polar bear: it is the Eskimo baby. The grandchildren of Nanook multiply prodigiously. The mothers kick-start their doughnut-wheeled tricycles and, arriving at their heated wooden houses, settle their children in front of the television. Destruction of the Eskimos, their reduction to a people of lost identity, is often predicted. But Eskimos are famously adaptable. They have endured formidable conditions but do not see their existence as harsh. Their land is where they, and the animals on which they depend, belong.

The word Eskimo means flesh-eater. Hunting has been the core of Eskimo existence. It is the means by which parents teach the young patience and responsibility. Eskimos say that if they do not eat caribou, seal and other wild food, they feel less well. The link between people and the animals that give them life is everywhere plain. Skins of bears, wolves and seals are pegged and stretched. Meat dries in the wind.

In the 1950s Eskimos were at low ebb, reduced by tuberculosis, alcohol and suicide. Canada built the schools and clinics that improved Eskimo education and health. An Eskimo leader said to me that his being sent away to be educated was the best thing that happened to him. 'We learned how to survive in the white world, a new discipline. Only education enables us to argue for our rights and remain Eskimo. It is also the best weapon against alcohol.'

Pang has a school, a clinic, a store, a community hall, a power generator, a Mounties police station. There is no bar or liquor shop. The people voted themselves dry. Their health is good.

Everything in the Arctic is expensive. The northern economy is strongly subsidised. But it is in Canada's interest. There is no alternative. Some Eskimo groups have found it difficult to keep to their traditions and culture. Pang's resourceful people are determined to remain strong. Since 1999 the vast traditional lands of the Inuit people of Arctic Canada have been known as Nunavut, meaning Our Land.

★

Andaman Islands, India, 1999. On the eastern side of the Bay of Bengal the Andaman Islands take shape. Looking through the Boeing's window, I see a scatter of jigsaw pieces in the haze. As we descend, I make out white beaches and eavesdropping palms. The plane swoops onto a short runway carved from red earth. This is Port Blair, the small capital of the islands. A taxi delivers me to a hotel by the harbour. The wharves are crowded with stained and dented freighters loading oil drums and sacks of rice. The air is scented with spice, diesel and salt water. Ferries beetle to and fro. All we need is Somerset Maugham in a white tropical suit. The Bay Island hotel has verandas perfect for eating, drinking and watching sunsets. The Andamans are a Union Territory of India and, although far to the east, they keep Indian time. Darkness falls like black velvet around six and the evening bazaar is lit by countless lamps.

The tribes of the Andamans were long ago named after Hanuman, the Hindu monkey god. In the Sherlock Holmes story *The Sign of Four*, the diabolical killer with a blowpipe is a tiny Andamanese.

One of the bustling ferries takes me to Viper Island. I walk the path through a coconut grove to a large domed red brick building on the hilltop. It houses a gallows. From 1858 the British raj turned the Andamans into a tropical gulag. Viper Island is only a part of it. At Port Blair the British built an immense stone jail to subdue Indian nationalism. Completed in 1906 it housed 600 prisoners, one to each cell. The first jailer was a harsh disciplinarian. The Andamans were the last stop for many Indians who opposed British rule. A three-man gallows and an iron flogging easel are still to be seen. One of the prisoners wrote of the comfort provided by a banyan tree. 'Under its shade one used to take breath after being flogged and tortured.' The last political prisoners left the jail in 1938 and the building is now a memorial.

I swim at an island called Jolly Buoy, snorkelling among swerving tropic shoals and blimpish fish with Garrick Club stripes. You can make your own holiday, boarding ferries on a whim and seeing what happens. The countryside is lush with lofty trees and great stands of coconut palms, banana patches, small wooden houses with verandas, bougainvillea and mooching cows. Of the 200 islands, thirty-eight are inhabited. Visitors are unlikely to see any of the aboriginal inhabitants, the four surviving tribes of small negroid people who traditionally lived as foragers in the forests. Only a few hundred survive the inevitably disastrous impact with the modern world. They have been reduced by fighting, disease, the spread of plantations, commercial tree-felling and the building of roads. Many have lost their culture and self-respect.

I went to Ross Island, the old British colonial settlement, and saw the eerie ruins, the officers' mess, governor's residence, houses and churches seized by jungle tentacles, half-digested by banyans. I swam and dived and wandered the beaches and rode the ferries of these remote islands. I cannot forget the brooding history.

★

Isla Negra, Chile, 2001. In Viŷa del Mar, on the coast of Chile, a man tried out his English on me. 'Why you come to Viŷa?' he asked. 'Weather or woman?'

'Wine,' I replied, 'and your famous flowers.'

He smiled. Viŷa takes pride in its kempt and beautiful subtropical gardens beside the ocean. 'Beach is nice in Viŷa,' he persisted. 'And woman on beach also.'

I was on my way to Isla Negra, near Valparaiso, to see the adored seaside home of Pablo Neruda, Chile's poet hero and at one time ambassador to France. As a merman manqué, he so loved the sea that he built his house on a bluff above the exploding surf and made it into Neptune's ante-room. He placed his bed diagonally in his bedroom so that he would awake facing the mighty Pacific. He kept his telescope handy on a bedside table. One morning he spied a ship's wooden hatch in the surf. He fished it out and gave it new life as a salty writing table.

He filled his home with shells and ships in bottles, books, charts and navigation equipment, model ships, musical instruments, and the long spiral tusk of a narwhal. Also a brooding figurehead of the Welsh pirate Henry Morgan.

His sense of humour led him to direct male guests to a little lavatory decorated with charming nudes in Victorian sepia photographs, the door adorned with fierce masks supposedly to frighten women away.

Neruda wrote his poetry in green ink, to his mind the colour of life. He won the Nobel Prize for Literature in 1971 and died in 1973. Pinochet's army and police damaged the house after Neruda's death. His friends restored it. He lies in a grave just below his enchanting home, where the surf falls in ceaseless cannonade.

★

Mexico City, 1992. At this altitude, 7,300 feet, a little tequila goes a long way. In the Opera Bar, cigarette smoke drifted from mirrored wooden booths where men and women took their animated ease. The crowded room, ornate, dark brown and ivory, was reflected in the mirror behind the counter, as in Manet's *A Bar at the Folies-Bergère*.

A guitarist, a violinist and a lugubrious bass player serenaded a woman. Her companion, who had paid for the tribute, looked into her dark eyes and joined the musicians in singing of love and longing. The woman stroked the back of his neck. Nearby, in seated tango, a middle-aged man with a Zapata moustache locked lips with a handsome woman with cascading curls. His rake's hand grasped her thigh and her own right hand drew his head closer to hers.

Street urchins sneaked through the door. Waiters shooed them away. As soon as they were broomed out, they scuttled in again to gaze at men taking tequila with a lick of salt. Sometimes they scrounged pesos, or were brushed off like flies. Musicians strummed a song of pity and unrequited love. The smoke rose to the high ceiling perforated by a single hole, an honoured hole, made by a bullet fired long ago by Pancho Villa, heroic revolutionary, the cruellest man who ever wore a sombrero.

I left the bar and walked to Garibaldi Square. Children slept in the hammocks of their mothers' laps or buttoned to the breast. Peppery vapours steamed from food stalls. Smoke floated through the batwing doors of a saloon which bore the notice: Entrance Forbidden to Persons Carrying Arms. Police hung around their patrol cars, hips jutting in macho poses to show off their guns. Professional troubadors swaggered in tight silvered trousers and jackets, stomachs cinched with silver-buckled belts, heads crowned with sombreros.

Men drove up to hire bands to play at a dinner or a party, and musicians scrambled like fighter pilots. Singers sang bittersweet words and melodies, the endless Mexican exploration of conflicted identity. Most of the country's 85 million people are of mingled Native Mexican and Spanish blood. They spring from the people of Native Mexican civilisations who were, as a Mexican suggested picturesquely to me, dusted with the pollen of Spanish bees: the gold-crazed conquistadores.

Almost five centuries after Hernán Cortés smashed the Aztec empire, the struggle to come to terms with a braided inheritance lies at the core of the Mexican condition. The Mexican is by heritage both taker and taken. There is a fascination with pale-skinned Spain as fatherland, yet many regard their root as Native Mexican, Mexico their brown-skinned motherland, and say to hell with Spain. Ambiguities of ancestry and the history of violence contribute to a brooding quality alongside fierce pride in the Mexican heart. Behind the scenery of fiesta and the dazzling colour of a creative people, the Native Mexican's solemn dignity consorts with the sombreness of Spain.

Mexico City is one of the most polluted places on earth and there is no possibility of improvement. For chilangos, as the city's inhabitants are called, there is simply no other place. It is a marvel.

A crowd gathered in prayer at a pink neon-lit shrine to the Virgin of Guadalupe. Drivers opened the bonnets of their trucks so that priests in white habits could sprinkle holy water over the engine. Market porters paused to have their barrows blessed. Enriqué, my guide, told me he had taken his car to church for a blessing.

I went to the house where Trotsky lived and where, in 1940, he was murdered on Stalin's order. The markets in Luganilla sell thousands of baby Jesus dolls, black, white and brown. They sell powders to bring luck to gamblers, a powder a girl sprinkles on her bosom to make her lost lover return, a destructor powder to sprinkle where your enemies are, for home or office use.

Enriqué and I were searched for weapons at a cantina devoted to the bullfight. A man shuffled from table to table. He was a salesman of pain. He carried an electric shock machine and his customers vied with each other in tests of machismo. In the Zona Rosa, a district of smart shops and restaurants, I dined in a pavement café. At the next table, a couple of middle-aged blades looked at the pretty girls walking by. I was aware of movement beneath the tables, crouching figures in the gloom. Boys tapped diners' ankles. Men placed their feet on boxes. The boys polished the diners' shoes until they gleamed like jewels. Coins were passed down. I heard a whispered 'gracias' from the shoeshine boys. Then they hopped away: the unprotesting poor, barely-seen, scratching a living in the teeming city.

Chapter 22

The vasty deep

'I've a little test for you.' It was the familiar voice of John Ridgway on the phone. He was about to set off on a voyage around the world in his ketch *English Rose VI*. He asked if I would like to join him on the Southern Ocean leg from Cape Town to Melbourne. I had no hesitation. 'Yes,' I said. I knew this would chime with one of his favourite maxims: 'The opportunity of a lifetime must be taken in the lifetime of the opportunity.' I had no doubt this would be a great adventure. I had a lot of work to cram into the next three months. I wrote the last chapter of a book and recorded a number of television and radio programmes. I arrived in Cape Town on 21 October. We sailed five days later.

It was nine o'clock on a cold morning. A gale howled. Outside the marina the angry sea rose and fell. But there could be no turning back now. A small crowd gathered to wish us luck. Aboard *English Rose* we cast off the warps tethering us to the dock. All except one. A renegade line jammed tightly, stubbornly umbilical. Nick Grainger darted forward and seized the knife in the mainmast scabbard. He severed the rope. It was so taut it made a bang like a pistol-shot. We bounced away into a monstrous swell and a forty-knot wind, surging through breaking wave tops, slithering down one side and climbing another.

The yacht club called us on the radio: 'Are you planning to return?' John Ridgway's grip on the wheel was a matter of might and main and formidable determination.

'No!' he shouted.

We fought our way out. Soon we were throwing up helplessly, standing in the cockpit, our arms around each other's shoulders. Two whales broke the surface for a look and dived at once with a shudder of tails.

We steered south-west to stay clear of the notorious ship-trap of the Agulhas bank. At last, the Cape of Good Hope fell astern. It was Saturday 25 October 2003, in the piercing cold spring of the Southern Ocean.

Three days later we crossed latitude 40 South and shaped for Melbourne, 6,100 nautical miles to the east, 7,000 land miles. Soon enough we would be in the relentless gales and the growling mountains of the seas. For the time being we contemplated the phosphorescent squid swirling by, the doodles of our wake, the jewels in the velvet of the night.

Curiosity drew the birds towards us, pistados and petrels and Antarctic prions. The first albatrosses ghosted in, balletic and sculptured, skimming the sea-slopes on long and elegant wings, seigneurial, wise and companionable. John is himself an honorary Wandering albatross. This stretch of the Southern Ocean, from the Cape to Melbourne, is the longest of his circumnavigation, the stormy albatross route across the lonely southern sea. One purpose of the voyage was to draw attention to the devastating slaughter of albatrosses by longline fishermen. The birds are attracted to the fish bait on lines many miles long and are killed by swallowing the hooks. John is robustly self-sufficient, master of his voyage, funding it himself, dedicating it to the albatrosses.

His affectionate name for *English Rose* is the old shippy. She has carried him on all his long-distance voyages for thirty years. She is fifty-seven feet long, twenty-nine tons and strong.

Sailing towards latitude 50 South, we were beyond help. We saw no ship, no sail, no mystery blob on the radar, no scratch of contrail in the sky. We sailed thousands of miles along the route to Australia pioneered by Victorian captains in their fast new ships. Until the 1850s, long-haul skippers bowed to Admiralty advice and stayed north of the roaring forties as they headed to Australian ports. The new oceanographers, John Towson, an Englishman, and Matthew Maury, an American, taught them to shorten and speed their voyages by steering great circle routes and harnessing the consistent and frequent westerly gales of the forties and fifties. In this manner they broke all records. In 1852 Captain James 'Bully' Forbes sailed the 2,500-ton *Marco Polo* from Liverpool to Melbourne with 930 migrant passengers in seventy-four days. This was a month faster than any previous voyage. Port officials believed Forbes only when he showed them the Liverpool newspapers he had bought on the day he sailed. 'Hell or Melbourne' was his cocky slogan. Two years later the Liverpool clipper *James Baines* reached Melbourne with 700 passengers and 180,000 letters in a record sixty-three days. Forbes returned from Melbourne in sixty-four days, a time never bettered. A story has it that Captain Richard Angel told his mate to put on more sail in a gale. 'Get the royals on her, and if you can't find anything else ask Mrs Angel to lend you her petticoat.'

Six of us sailed in *English Rose*. John and Marie Christine occupied the cabin on the port quarter. Nick Grainger, Igor Asheshov and Quentin Hanich had fo'c'sle bunks. Nick was a genial and lanky Australian academic, a skilled sailor and computer wizard. Igor was forty, an amiable Russian-English-Peruvian. Quentin was an Australian Greenpeacenik of thirty-three. Perhaps we had differing reasons for being out here but mostly, I think, we sailed for adventure's sake.

My berth on the starboard side of the saloon was a marsupial nook with bedsocks. The thick sleeping bag had an inner silk sack. I wore thermal underwear at all times. There was no heating on board. John declared the human body warm enough. If seaboot socks were wet and icy, he said, 'stick them in your armpits when you get into your bunk and they'll be dry when you wake up'. This turned out to be right.

Waking around seven in the morning, I took a vacuum flask from the galley, my hot water ration of seven-tenths of a litre. In the head, the tiny bathroom in the bow, I devoted half my water to a shave and a flannel wash. For this wash I followed the formula of a friend in Wales who was taught it by his mother when he first went camping. 'Wash down as far as possible, wash up as far as possible, then wash possible.' As the yacht corkscrewed and the bow fell like a forge hammer, I performed a feat of balance with the razor but sometimes emerged a slightly bloodied Blondin. The remaining half of my water ration brewed my tea and rendered my cereal chewable.

We divided into three watches. Quentin was my watch mate. We steered the yacht from two to four in the morning, from ten in the morning to two in the afternoon, from eight to ten in the evening.

I started dressing fifteen or twenty minutes before the watch began. Grabbing handholds and hopping from foot to foot, I pulled a padded suit over my thermals, then struggled into the outer oilskin layer of salopettes, a high collar red coat, socks and boots, a balaclava, cap, gloves and mittens. I climbed the companionway into the doghouse, leading to the cockpit and steering wheel. John and Marie Christine were pleased to see me: they would be in their bunks in a few minutes. When I arrived for the two to four morning watch on 31 October, they smiled and said: 'Look.' For the first time, I saw the aurora australis, the sky theatrical, green and red, like a painting by Turner, one of the attractions of being aboard.

Two stout rope tethers fastened me to the cockpit and secured me at the wheel. My harness lifeline was clipped to a jackstay, a safety line. Steering in heavy weather, I kept the compass course and a look out. It was a matter of total concentration, especially in the dark. The wind howled and shrieked and the waves arrived in uproar, barging like bears into the cockpit.

This was the wildest place I had ever been. Wind and waves were more formidable than any I experienced in Atlantic weather. Gale followed upon gale, the southern seas rolling lordly and unimpeded. They were impressively striking in their power and immensity, their height, their thunder, their dark blue bulk etched with white marble veins. At three in the morning of 3 November, at latitude 44 South, a storm carried away the self-steering gear, our robot coxswain. It overwhelmed the electronic autopilot. Now, keeping our grasp on the wheel, we would have to steer manually every mile to Melbourne. The wind rose to fifty knots and more, a roaring Force 11, right on the bow. We could sail no longer. The wheel was lashed to leeward and a small patch of the staysail was set. The yacht lay safely a-try, moving very slowly. Snow settled in drifts on the deck and doghouse. Ice chunks tumbled from the masts and thudded on the deck.

Amid this mayhem, Marie Christine cooked and ducked the flying pans. No one else could use the galley. Baked beans and bread make a perfect feast in a storm. When the battle became quieter she cooked potatoes, pasta, cabbage and corned beef, or made our day with a famous haggis. We ate the last bananas on day nine, but still had South

African oranges, apples and pineapple. 'I can't say I love sailing,' Marie Christine said, 'it's often horrible. The fact is – I love John and he's a persuasive man.'

We saw the distant snowcapped mountains of the Prince Edward Islands. As I finished a spell at the wheel, Ridgway asked cheerily: 'Everything all right?' 'I don't know what's worse,' I said, 'the fear or the terror.'

When my watch was over, I went below to the saloon to step out from my oilskins. How I loved the sound of Velcro in the morning, ripping open the fastenings of the outer and inner suits, hanging up the wet outerwear to drip and dry, then wriggling into the kapok for instant sleep.

The ocean grew rougher, the air colder. The sleet was stinging. The yacht tobogganed down the waves. Keeping the course was demanding. Crossing the 60th meridian we changed our clock to GMT + 5. A flock of petrels, prions and albatrosses joined us for the boisterous ride towards Kerguelen. The weather's cold grip was relentless. Our latitude was almost 50 South and we were on the Antarctic convergence where the cold Antarctic sea meets the warmer Southern Ocean.

Standing in the cockpit, looking through binoculars, I saw the island of Kerguelen seven miles distant, the halfway point in our voyage. The Rendezvous Rock at the western end rose 280 feet out of the sea, streaked with guano. The regimented swells hammered the cliffs in spectacular explosions of spray. Captain Cook reached Kerguelen on 24 December 1776. He called it Desolation Island. Rain or snow falls here on 300 days a year.

As John took his turn at the wheel, a Wandering albatross with a handsome roman bill flew close to his shoulder. The bird was unafraid, its eyes assessed the skipper. It kept station with effortless and subtle flicks of slim and graceful wings, spanning seven or eight feet or more. Albatrosses live to be more than sixty and maybe this one was as old as John, who was sixty-five. These birds are thought to refer to the moon and stars in their navigation; considering the old seafarers' belief that such birds are sailors' souls, I fancied that the albatross at John's shoulder was checking the cockpit compass. The eyes of albatross and man met in contemplative gaze, each recognizing a kindred wanderer.

We liked them in their role of ocean escorts, outriders, good company, skimming down broad waves, settling on the sea to rest, folding their wings in graceful origami.

John used his daily blog to take up the cause of the threatened albatrosses. In their odysseys, they spend most of their life on the ocean. They travel phenomenal distances in search of squid and krill, thousands of miles in a single journey, perhaps 500 miles in a day, their wings seemingly tireless as they soar at sixty miles an hour and more.

We entered a fjord of quiet and pearly water on Kerguelen's sheltered south-eastern side. Penguins patrolled and dolphins showed us their high-speed sporting tricks. Elephant seals snorted like colonels in a club. A crowd of the small albatrosses called mollymawks assembled for a meeting. At Port aux Français we made fast to a large buoy. Few yachts call here: maybe one a year. A boat buzzed us to the French scientific settlement, a place of blue, green and cream huts, workshops, laboratories, a hospital and a pocket church.

We luxuriated in the showers. Later we talked to the naturalists about their studies of albatrosses. In the world's remotest French restaurant, we lunched on soup, chicken, macaroni, cheese and exquisite coffee. Igor told me later that after our lunch a French girl sweetly gave him a little red wine and a kiss. Our arms filled with fresh long loaves, we returned to *English Rose*.

Now we set sail. We were 3,150 nautical miles from Melbourne, an Atlantic away. We looked back at Kerguelen's snowy peaks. They rose to 6,000 feet and formed a mysterious *Lord of the Rings* backdrop. Glancing over our shoulders, we saw the mountains for a couple of hours. A gale set in and we shortened sail to help Marie Christine cook more easily. Flocks of birds pursued us in the manner of gulls behind a plough. Mars presided after sunset. There were swarming stars. A cheesy yellow quarter moon rose very low. Soon it was business as usual, a cold night and the ocean's attrition. Our reliable friends Sirius and Orion's Belt helped us on our way.

We had a bright dawn, a gale, a rough wet day and cold hands and feet. The next day, too, was comfortless and wet; the day after that, a rogue sea gave us a punch and the pots flew in the galley and many eggs were cracked. Marie Christine changed the menu to omelettes and said with some feeling: 'I hate the boat, hate it.'

Next day we had another helping of violence, a Force 10 storm and waves full of temper. As it increased to Force 11, the spray streamed horizontally and approaching seas rumbled like Tube trains in a tunnel. Marauding waves landed blows on our backs. Seawater seethed in the cockpit, silver and sapphire, gurgling its way through the drains. Squalls and gales raged all week and we longed for a glimpse of blue. We moved cautiously, slowly and stiffly in our oilskin armour, edging more like crabs than humans.

And then, one morning, our spirits bubbled. *English Rose* picked up her skirts and danced. It was an interval as lovely as it was short-lived. Another gale was soon upon us. In the doghouse log book the skipper noted: 'Rough. Reaching across a big sea.' Our wrestling with the wheel made our wrists and fingers ache, storing up twinges for our old age.

John encouraged us to decorate the doghouse log with drawings, cartoons and verses. I took my doggerel for a walk and wrote: 'I've letters here, the Postman calls, for Mr Gale and Mr Squalls. And Mr Frost and Mr Snow, and Messrs Sleet and Hail and Blow.'

More usefully, I repaired the wet and disintegrating logbook with scarlet gaffer tape. Running before rough seas, we found a split in the mainsail. We could no longer set it. In the first days of December the bad weather abated and Marie Christine mended a rip in the mizzen staysail with stitches and tape.

And then, quite suddenly, we were becalmed. The sea undulated gently. It looked more prairie than ocean. Mollymawks sat on the water like bathtime ducks. The following day we removed our oilskin coats for the first time since we left Cape Town. The silken sea was barely rippled. A shark prowled for a while and mooched off. I drew a cartoon of the yacht becalmed, flaccid sails mirrored in the ocean, and a speech bubble: 'Who shot the albatross?'

On 11 December, Nick rang the yacht's bronze bell to signal our farewell to the roaring forties. We were 600 miles from Melbourne and heading for a dangerous coast punctuated by wrecked ships.

Two hundred miles from Melbourne, the numbers of black petrels and little storm petrels and our flock of prions drifted away. Our faithful albatrosses, our pilots, seemed to say farewell one by one, like workers clocking out. We were sorry to see them go. Theirs was the southern sea and the unremitting gales.

A little before midnight on 14 December, we saw the spark of the lighthouse at Cape Otway, guarding the headland at the approach to Melbourne. Lights glimmered and twinkled in distant coastal villages. Moonlight dappled the inky sea. We smelled the faint scent of gum trees and warm earth, the delectable sniff of the land. On a sunny Sunday morning we jostled in cross currents and whirlpools through the narrow entrance to Port Phillip, sailing on an artist's broad blue bay stippled with fishing craft and sloopy sailing boats. In the distance rose the misty smudge of the city's towers. We sailed for six hours to cross the harbour to our berth. We were fifty-one days out of Cape Town.

Ashore at last, I looked at the old shippy. Ours had been adventure unforgettable. Among the wild orchestrations of the ocean and its insistent voices, its roaring and wailing and thunderous drums, we learned something of the sea and also of our small selves. I think of it often.

Index

Other books by the author

Wales and the Welsh

Talking of Wales

Americans and Nothing Else

India File: Inside the Subcontinent

The State of America

Out of Red Darkness

My Foreign Country

Cobra Road: an Indian Journey

Conquerors of Time: Exploration and Invention in the Age of Daring

Wild Tracks, More Wild Tracks, Sea Stories, More Sea Stories

In this Place: National Library of Wales

Senedd

Pembrokeshire: Journeys and Stories

A Gift of Sunlight: The fortune and quest of the Davies sisters of Llandinam

SPACE SHUTTLE

TREVOR FISHLOCK
THE TIMES/LONDON

511

POLICE DEPARTMENT

1984
WORKING
PRESS
2755

DAILY TELEGRAPH

PRO OP-ED

exFishlock, Cape Canaveral, May 10

SPACE

Cape Canaveral

    Along Florida ce Coast the pulse quickens.
two and a half er the Challenger disaster
prepares to p pace again. Next week th
for a shuttl e delivered here. But
the bustle. a people glad to be
business w, there is an un
uncertai mme's future.
Increas space.

7
1986
TEXAS PRISON RODEO

It Takes Guts!
Come see the toughest cowboys in Texas.

WORKING PRESS

Trevor Fishlock May 10 89

graph FeaturesFor Trevor Grove

Texas Bangs. Bootleg. Blowout. Bonanza. Bronco. In the place names of Texas there
is history and rough poetry. John Wayne might have been sheriff in burgs like
Stagecoach, Stampede, Geronimo, Gunsight, Pointblank, Cut and Shoot,
and Fort Spunky. There are specks of towns with short jabs of name
Fred, Frog, Grit, Gus, Joy, Jud, Nix, Pep, Uz. And entertainment
Pancake, Dime Box, Juno, Noodle, Bug Tussle, Hoop a Holla
and Ding Dong in Bell County. Every name tells a Texan ta
and Telephone, Petrol m and Uncertain, Happy, Lovin
High Chaparral and Weeping Mary.
  In the evocative litany of American names the Texas
with the most curiosities.
  To Texans this is as fitting as it is obvious. The theory
Texianism, founded on the premise that what is Texan i
demands the trumpeti the c
encapsulating th
Texas, our grea
an braggado

CHRSTAIR
VXP
PARCKNINTURN

C.S.C.E.
Sommet de Paris
1990

P
FISHLOCK
TREVOR
DAILY